The Complete Book of GYMNASTICS

David Hunn

CHARTWELL BOOKS INC.

① Secaucus, N.J.
②
③ 1979. c.1978
④ 200p

Published by Chartwell Books Inc.
A Division of Book Sales Inc.
110 Enterprise Avenue
Secaucus, New Jersey 07094

First published in USA in 1979

© Ward Lock 1978

Published in Great Britain in 1978
by Ward Lock Limited, London,
a member of the Pentos Group.

Printed in United States of America

1. Gymnastics

We are grateful to the following for
kindly providing photographs for this
book.

Colour photographs:
E. D. Lacey page 49; Allsport/Tony
Duffy pages 50, 66; Allsport/Don Morley
page 65; Colorsport pages 133, 152; Peter
Moeller page 134; Gerry Cranham,
jacket, and page 151.

Black and white photographs:
Peter Moeller pages 7, 8, 9, 29, 34, 35,
56, 57 right, 58, 63 left, 76, 77, 78, 80,
86, 91, 105, 108 right, 109, 113 below,
115, 125, 126 top and below left, 127, 155
left, 157; Popperfoto/UPI pages 13, 22
left, 24, 28 right, 53; Allsport/Tony
Duffy pages 14, 27 left, 31, 32, 33, 61,
114, 117 below, 120, 126 below right,
129, 161; Allsport/Mark Moylan pages
26, 30 below, 46, 85, 121 left, 137, 155
right, 160; Allsport page 30 above;
Syndication International page 25;
Colorsport pages 11, 16, 17, 20, 22 right,
23, 27 right, 28 left, 42, 43, 44, 45, 47,
48, 51, 55, 57 left, 60, 63 right, 68, 71,
73, 74, 75, 82, 84, 88, 90, 93, 95, 96, 99,
100, 101, 102, 103, 108 left, 110, 113,
above, 117 above, 121 right, 122, 123,
124, 128, 131, 136, 138, 139, 141, 145.

We are grateful to the *Fédération
Internationale de Gymnastique* for the
material in Chapter 20.

Line illustrations by Drawing Attention/
Rhoda/Robert Burns.

Contents

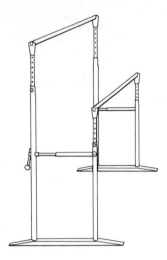

Gymnastics apparatus
From above – left: rings (men); vaulting horse (men); balance beam (women); from above – centre: pommel horse (men); horizontal bar, or high bar (men); parallel bars (men); from above – right; asymmetric bars (women); vaulting horse (women).

4

Foreword

You will not need to be an expert to enjoy this book, nor even a competitor, and neither will age be a barrier: that's what pleased me about it most of all. There have been many books on gymnastics written in the past few years, aimed at beginners, advanced gymnasts, coaches, judges – all crammed with helpful technical detail, but not all exactly readable; all packed with pictures of gymnastic perfection, or the nearest that could be found to it, with expert analysis of the movements and how they could be achieved.

What David Hunn has done in 'The Complete Book of Gymnastics' has not, I think, been done before. He has covered just about the entire field of gymnastic activity, not merely the best-known part of it, and covered the work in it of both males and females. Such chapters as those on sports acrobatics and modern rhythmic gymnastics are unusual, and so particularly welcome. So is his history of the sport and, as an Olympic competitor, it was exciting for me to find the Games at Munich and Montreal recreated in such detail. The photographs are simply splendid, some of the best I have seen, and were obviously chosen for that reason, not just for their instructional value.

Sensibly, the book does not dwell on the improbability that every gymnast could be a champion, or even wants to be. It attempts to take the interested spectator as well as the initiated convert through the sport from beginning to end. I found it easily readable and most interesting, and I hope that anyone who reads this foreword will agree with me that this book *is* gymnastics.

Avril Lennox
(British champion 1974–77)

Introduction

Since the extraordinary explosion of both participant and spectator interest in gymnastics set off by Olga Korbut during the 1972 Olympic Games, the sport – and particularly the female side of it – has been knee-deep in books of instruction. Excellent though many of them are, there has, strangely enough, hardly been one that covered both men's and women's gymnastics; nor one that devoted more than token space to the history of the sport and to the peripheral but rapidly-growing activities of trampolining, tumbling, sports acrobatics and modern rhythmic gymnastics, as well as the place in the sport of educational gymnastics.

In *The Complete Book of Gymnastics* I have tried to open all these doors to explore what lies within. This is not a comprehensive book of technical instruction, though with the expert guidance of Avril Lennox, the outstanding British gymnast of the past decade, it does, we both hope, give some helpful insight to the basics and the polished craftsmanship of every part of the sport.

I was particularly anxious that the book should be one that the follower of gymnastics (like me) should find interesting and entertaining. To this end the exciting elements of the gymnastic routines have been described from the point of view of the spectator rather than the performer, and biographical notes on many of the world's leading performers in recent years have been included.

The bibliography at the end of this book indicates the range of my research, and inevitably I drew assistance from many previously published works. More than on any others, I fell with relief on the American work *Olympic Gymnastics for Men and Women,* the most comprehensive single volume hitherto published on the practice of this sport. Dennis Horne's excellent *Trampolining* answered many of my queries on that subject, and is thoroughly recommended to those who seek such expertise. Among the individuals without whom I should have been lost, none was more helpful than the sports acrobatics expert, Pat Wade, and none suffered longer than my typist, Jenny Hollow.

David Hunn
Yapton, Sussex, England

1 The Story of Gymnastics

No sport is so closely linked with the development of man as gymnastics. For uncharted centuries, the ancient civilizations of China, Persia and India embraced physical activities that were collected and refined by the Greeks, from whose language the word was formed. Gymnastics meant almost as much to their great culture as did music and art; they believed that the coordination of mind and body was improved by general physical development, and that the human body could increase in size, strength and aptitude in proportion to the use made of it. Gymnastics became, to the ancient Greeks, not only a greatly-admired form of exercise, but an important part of education, an integral thread of life.

It seems unlikely that any form of pure gymnastics was ever included in the ancient Olympic Games, which were held every four years from 776 BC to 393 AD, but gymnasia were of great significance in Greece in that time. The Greek word for naked is *gymnos*, and certainly most of the physical activities in the building were carried on without the encumbrance of clothing. (So were most athletic events of the ancient Games from 720 BC, when the winner of the stadium race is said to have lost his shorts on the way round.) But the gymnasia, which were state built and supervised, also housed the local school and included rooms for art

The women's World Cup trophies, first competed for in London in 1975. An individual contest between the world's top gymnasts, it is now held every two years

7

'Friendship first, competition second' is the firm slogan of all Chinese sportsmen, nowhere more evident than with their touring gymnasts

and music. They were used for public meetings and were the gathering places of the philosophers and intellectuals of the town. Different schools of philosophy grew up in different gymnasia – in Athens, Plato was to be found at the Academy, Aristotle at the Lyceum.

Each centre appointed *gymnastae*, a combination of teacher, coach and trainer, and was ruled by a *gymnasiarch*. In 500 BC Athens had ten such men, who were responsible for conducting sports and games at all the public festivals, for supervising the competitors, morally as well as physically, and for directing the schools.

Gradually, the predominant place occupied in Greek life by athleticism and youthful ideals gave way to the power of philosophy and rhetoric. The glory of physical competition faded, and was largely replaced by more aggressive confrontation. Alexander the Great and the Macedonians were devoted to conquest in war, not peace; the Roman Empire was built on the disciplines not of the gymnasium, but of the barracks, and it was not particularly surprising that their only lasting contribution to the gymnastic world was the development of exercises on the wooden horse, which their soldiers used to practise mounting and dismounting, and from which today's vaulting horse and pommel horse evolved. The Greeks were great participants, the Romans great spectators. They turned the athletic stadia into barbarous amphitheatres. Finally, the death knell of gymnastics and all festivals of sport was sounded with the rise of the early Christians – the body was not to be worshipped. It was the prison of the soul, and punishment and torture were its lot.

Twice world and once Olympic overall champion, the enchanting Ludmilla Tourischeva was never short of admirers in whatever part of the world she visited

When she was Soviet Junior Champion, Olga Koval appeared on the British television programme 'Blue Peter'. She fell during her routine and carried on without a murmur

More than 1500 years passed before the Olympics were revived, but gymnastics awoke in Germany in the late 18th century, where the idea was nurtured of building the body for strength, rather than beauty. The most influential leader of that concept was Johann (Kurt) Jahn, who opened the Turnplatz, an open-air gymnasium near Berlin in 1811, the modern world's first such centre. Jahn created the parallel bars and the horizontal bar, and did much to promote the sport as a club activity throughout Europe, by sending groups of gymnasts on exhibition tours. By the middle of the 19th century, German immigrants in the United States of America were establishing something similar, called *turnvereins*, and even women had taken to the parallel bars.

Jahn's muscular philosophy was in direct contrast to that of his contemporary, Per Henrik Ling, the father of Swedish gymnastics. Ling was devoted to free expression in gymnastics, which he viewed as part of the educational system, teaching rhythm and fluency of movement. The whole German concept of gymnastics came under fire and the battle between the two camps continued for two generations. It focussed particularly on the parallel bars (in Germany, the controversy was known as the *barren-*

kampf). Some of Ling's most vociferous supporters claimed that the bars were endangering health by causing muscular and anatomical deformation. Apart from which, said one, 'they degrade the human body to the level of a mechanical pendulum and an instrument of senseless movement'.

Today, both branches of the tree are part of modern gymnastics, but you will still find people within the sport who cling firmly to one, rather than the other. Physical training of some kind found its way on to the curriculum of many European schools during the Victorian era, and in Britain the sport received a considerable boost in 1860, when the Army officially adopted it. The Army Gymnastic Staff was formed (later the Army Physical Training Corps) from twelve NCOs, and from that moment to this the British Army has never lost its enthusiasm for, and success in, the sport.

Gymnastics were firmly enough established internationally for them to be included in the first celebration of the modern Olympic Games, in Athens in 1896. Prizes were awarded to the first and second in each event: a diploma, silver medal and crown of olive branches for the winner; a diploma, bronze medal and crown of laurel for the runner-up. Germans won three of the six gymnastic events and were second in three. Floor exercises for men, definitely not part of the German approach, were not held, but rope-climbing was included. Women were not invited to compete until 1928, when there was a team competition only; astonishingly, there were no individual female events until 1952.

In those 1896 Olympics, there was no combined individual prize. Had there been, it would surely have gone to the German, Hermann Weingartner, who won the high bar, was second in the rings and the pommel, and third in the parallel bars. In the next Olympiad, oddly enough, the only gymnastic prize was for the combined exercises, a mighty test of an athlete. They comprised today's six items plus rope climbing, long and high jump combined, pole vault and having a weight of 110 lb (49.8 kg). The first five places went to Frenchmen (the 1900 Games were held in Paris). In 1904, the Americans staged the Olympics, in St Louis, and swept the board, or very nearly. Few Europeans were prepared to travel such a vast distance: only twelve nations competed, compared to twenty-two in Paris, and of the 617 athletes, only fifty-one were not from North America. The United States of America provided 107 of the 119 gymnastic competitors, and they were kept extraordinarily busy. Apart from a team combined event, there were ten separate events for individuals. Of these, one was a nine-event combination, another a seven-event apparatus combination, and a third a triathlon comprising long jump, shot put and 100-yard sprint. Americans won almost everything in sight, including first three places in the team event. The combined individual winner was an Austrian, Julius Lenhardt, who by virtue of being a student at the University of Philadelphia was a member of an American team.

Italy soon emerged as one of the world's most successful gymnastic nations, led by the superb Alberto Braglia, and despite the rising challenge of the Swiss and the Swedes, won four of the five Olympiads between 1912 and 1932. Not surprisingly, Germany pulled out the stops for the Berlin Olympics of 1936 and returned to the top of the gymnastic tree as champions of the combined individual event, and both men's and women's team events.

During the decades between the world wars, gymnastics was again torn between the Swedish style (free expression without apparatus) and the German (devoted to fixed apparatus exercises), with two new facets of the sport beginning to show themselves: flexible strength from Denmark, with clubs and dumbbells to the fore, and rhythmic gymnastics with music from France, which England and the USA called recreative gymnastics. Sometimes associated with particular branches of gymnastics, and sometimes not, the debate raged on as to whether gymnastics was or should be a sport, or whether it was and should remain a part of the physical education programme.

In Britain, there was a notable decline in interest in gymnastics in this vital period between the wars, largely because of its Germanic associations. Physical educationalists, in particular, recoiled from the muscular stress that appeared to be created by apparatus gymnastics. A rift persisted between the British Amateur Gymnastics Association (founded in 1888) and the state Board of Education, and for many years it restricted British progress in the competitive side of the sport. All in all, there was a desperate need for one international authority to blend and standardize the aims and execution of gymnastics, and the FIG (International Gymnastic Federation) had its hands full.

The Second World War had an extraordinary effect on gymnastics. On the one hand, it totally halted competitive development in all but neutral countries (note that in the 1948 Olympics, Finland won five gymnastic gold medals and Switzerland three). On the other hand, the vital need for physical fitness throughout the armed forces of the warring world, and the high degree to which that was developed in key sections such as the commando units, revealed the delights and benefits of that sport to more adults than had ever contemplated them before.

In the Los Angeles Olympics of 1932, only seven nations contested the gymnastic events, although admittedly the Games were held at a time of acute world depression; at Helsinki in 1952 there were 319 competitors from twenty-nine nations, and there was a full programme of women's individual events, as well as the team competition. The astonishing feat of those Games was the overwhelming success of the Soviet gymnasts, competing for the first time. They won the men's and women's team and combined individual events, as well as three of the men's and two of the women's solo championships. The great Viktor Chukarin took gold medals in the combined event, the pommel and the vault, and silvers in the rings and parallel bars. It was no surprise that the USSR showed they could hold their own in the gymnasium, but that they should have dominated the competition was a total surprise. It was later learned that when their gymnasts were shown a film of the German

Nobody in the history of gymnastics has captivated as many hearts as Olga Korbut, who caused many to forget that she never won a major all-round title

triumphs of 1936, it caused more amusement than admiration.

That was not the only remarkable feature of the 1952 Olympics. The Japanese, who had competed without much success in 1948, had really gone to work. They too had been studying film of all the leading gymnasts, and in Helsinki they came up with a silver medal in the men's floor exercises, and second, third and fourth places in the men's vault. Two more individuals are worth noting: Alfred Schwarzmann (Germany), who had been the all-round champion sixteen years earlier, was still good enough to win a silver on the high bar; he shared it with the acclaimed master of that piece of equipment, Josef Stalder of Switzerland, originator of the Stalder Shoot and the gold medallist of 1948.

The first world championships had been held by then, in 1950 at Basle, where the Swiss won seven of the eight men's titles. It was the last time the western world laid a hand on a championship: from that moment men's gymnastics settled down to being what it has remained ever since – a relentless struggle for supremacy between the USSR and Japan. The world championships of 1954, in Rome: Chukarin shares the title with his team-mate Muratov, and the USSR take five of the seven men's gold medals and four of the six women's; Japan take the other two men's titles. Melbourne Olympics of 1956: in the first ten places of the combined individual event, there are five Soviet and four Japanese gymnasts. Chukarin wins the title from Takashi Ono by five-hundredths of a point, becoming the first gymnast for forty years to win the championship twice. Four years later, Ono was again defeated, by Shakhlin of the USSR, by 0.05 – how he must have longed for one extra stroke of perfection in just one exercise!

Since the entry of the Soviet Union to women's gymnastics, only one other nation has ever won a world or Olympic women's team title. Year after year they go on producing not one great gymnast, but a handful of them. The end of one superb artist only makes way for another, and to measure the

queen of one era against the queen of another is as difficult a task in gymnastics as in lawn tennis, ice skating, or acting. Today there is certainly closer competition at the very top than there was twenty years ago, which is why one cannot look merely at the gold medals won by Larissa Semyonovna Latynina and say 'There stood the greatest of them all.' You will not, however, find many to argue against you.

It was at Melbourne that she reached the top. Her detailed career record will be found among the biographies in Chapter 4; for the moment, suffice it to say that in three Olympics she won nine gold, five silver and three bronze medals, and was twice the individual all-round champion, and twice, in 1958 and 1962, the overall world champion.

With the Soviet Union apparently unassailable on the throne of women's gymnastics, it was all to the good that Japan's men continued their incredible progress. In Rome in 1960, they filled six of the first nine places and took the Olympic team title for the first time. They have never lost it, incessantly producing a whole troop of performers so brilliant they are almost interchangeable. Ono, Endo, Kato, Nakayama, Tsukahara – where do you stop? The Japanese performance in Rome opened a new door in gymnastic history, demonstrating a standard of complexity and of sheer elegance never before touched. Shakhlin, the world champion, just took the individual Olympic title from Ono, but it was sixteen years before that returned to the USSR.

Yukio Endo won the overall title in front of his home crowd at the 1964 Olympics, though by then Titov (USSR) was the world champion. This was the occasion on which Yamashita displayed what was to

High bar winner in the first World Cup was Japan's legendary Mitsuo Tsukahara, twice Olympic champion. Second was Gienger (Germany) and third Kajiyama (Japan)

become the most famous vault in the world. It was also the occasion on which the beautiful Czech, Vera Caslavska, supplanted Latynina as Olympic and later world champion. Thanks to the brilliant efforts of Caslavska and her comrades in these and the next Olympics, the Soviet Union on each occasion were within one point of losing the team championship.

By 1964, television techiques and its sales across the world were such that gymnastics began to acquire an international audience of staggering proportions. In Mexico, in 1968, women's gymnastics in particular was somewhat astonished to find itself besieged by fans, thousands of whom were anguished to be turned away from the packed Muni-

cipal Auditorium every day. Despite the historic 'Fosbury Flop' high jump and some startling track performances, Caslavska was the unforgettable star of the Games. She shone as never before, winning four gold medals and then marrying a Czech runner before returning to Prague. Sawao Kato (Japan) succeeded Endo as men's Olympic champion, though again only by the magical five-hundredths of a point over the Soviet champion, Voronin – whose wife, Voronina, was only 0.6 behind Caslavska. The 19-year-old Soviet hope, Kuchinskaya, fell from the asymmetric bars to finish 0.1 down on her compatriot. The men's reigning floor champion, Menichelli (Italy), fell at the end of his routine on the mat and snapped an Achilles tendon.

Kuchinskaya was expected to succeed Caslavska as the queen of gymnastics, but serious illness prevented that. The Czech's retirement, at 26, let in another great Soviet artist, Ludmilla Tourischeva. She took the next world and Olympic championships, hotly pursued by East Germans, but if you asked the twenty million television viewers who was the female star of the Munich Olympics, there is no doubt at all what the answer would be: Olga Korbut. Whether in tears or smiles, her elfin figure and vibrant personality captivated the greatest audience gymnastics had ever had. Single-handed, she was responsible for the immense boom in girls' gymnastics through the 70s, as millions of children queued to sign on at their nearest club. Though she won gold medals on the beam and floor, and a silver on the bars, Korbut finished only seventh overall. Never have judges been less popular!

The men were so overshadowed that Kato's great performance in becoming the third man in history to take the overall title

twice was hardly noticed by the public. Apart from walking away with the team championship, Japan this time secured all three places on the podium in the combined exercises results.

In Montreal, in 1976, the Soviet Union struck back. A young man named Nikolai Andrianov joined the immortals by winning the floor, vault and rings and finishing a full point ahead of Kato overall. The bronze medal went to Mitsuo Tsukuhara, whose startling new vault brought him top marks in the optional section, but in the team competition the Japanese finished less than half a point up on the USSR. Once again, though, it was an elfin who took the watch-

ing world by storm: 14-year-old Nadia Comaneci became the first Romanian to win a gymnastic gold medal in Olympic history – and she made sure of a place in the record books by winning the beam with 19.95 out of a possible 20, winning the asymmetric bars with the first all-perfect marks ever given in Olympic gymnastics, and beating Nelli Kim and Tourischeva to the overall championship. It was an unbelievable performance, and it took Romania into second place in the team competition, behind (of course) the USSR.

2 1972: Korbut at Munich

None of us who lived through the Munich Olympics will ever forget its horror – the death of seventeen men, eleven of them Israeli hostages. Almost as inevitably, it is difficult to banish its principal joy – a minute Soviet waif named Olga Korbut. What she unwittingly did for gymnastics cannot be overestimated, though many people within the sport have been aggravated by the emphasis given by the media to that contribution. The fact is that in Britain, for example, gymnastics did not live as a public sport until after 1972. What gave it life was Olga Korbut – and television.

For British sports journalists in Munich that August, gymnastics had very low priority indeed, despite the presence of three British male competitors – Wild, Arnold and Norgrove and a full team of six women – in the order in which they finished: Hutchinson, Willett, Alred, Lennox, Hopkins and Mugridge. There was absolutely no expectation of British success, but what was more to the point, there was no Vera Caslavska, the brilliant and beautiful Czech who had reigned in Tokyo and Mexico. Neither were her closest rivals from 1968 still in the hunt, Voronina and Kuchinskaya of the Soviet Union. For all its devastating efficiency, men's gymnastics was not – and even now, is not – quite such a crowd-puller, so it was understandable that when the gymnastic programme got under way in the *Sporthalle* on the first day of the Games, Sunday 27 August, British journalists scarcely gave it a thought.

Television cameras, however, were in attendance, and it was not long before the press were puzzled to receive abrupt telex messages from newspaper head offices: 'Must cover Korbut,' 'Interview Korbut soonest,' 'Korbut pix most urgent.' The truth was that few of us even knew in what sport Korbut was competing, nor from what nation, and there was at least one distinguished correspondent who was so convinced his editor was potty that he consigned the message to the bin and proceeded as before. As we all know now, they had got it right at home: Olga Korbut was a star, the star of the Games. Television had allowed this little imp to fill twenty million sitting rooms in Britain alone, and heaven knows how many others elsewhere.

When I was first sent off to go 'doorstepping' for Korbut – the awful practice whereby a reporter sits on the relevant doorstep till his quarry crosses it, one way or the other – I stood aside to let her pass. Though the girl wore a USSR track suit, it was quite clear to me that she was somebody's infant daughter, certainly no more than 12 years old. The mistake was almost excusable: though Korbut was then 17, she was only 4 ft 11 ins tall, bustless, and weighed no more than six stone. But already this little sparrow – originally only in the Soviet team at Munich as a reserve – had sent half the world wild.

The USSR had won every women's Olympic team prize since they first entered, at Helsinki in 1952, but this time – though

TOP: With the strain already showing, Olga Korbut and Soviet team coach Larissa Latynina wait for scores on one of Korbut's unhappy days at the Munich Games

ABOVE: Even her East German rival Erika Zuchold can hardly believe the bitter truth. For Korbut another golden Olympic dream had crashed. But she was only fifteen

few believed they would be beaten – there was just a chance that the German Democratic Republic (East Germany) might do it: they still had their outstanding competitors Erika Zuchold and Karin Janz, fourth and sixth in Mexico. The USSR had only Ludmilla Tourischeva and Liubov Burda with Olympic experience, and in Mexico they were placed 24th and 25th.

The extraordinarily complicated structure and scoring of the Olympic gymnastic contest is detailed later in the book. Suffice it for now to say that the team competition comes first, in which all six members compete in all events, first at a compulsory exercise and next with a voluntary one of their own creation – the optional exercise, as it is known. The lowest score of each team in each exercise is disregarded, and the teams are placed by the sum of their remaining scores in the eight exercises (for men, twelve exercises). The scores of individuals in this part of the competition are collated to determine the winner of the individual all-round (or combined exercises) championship.

It was immediately apparent that this was once again going to be a battle between the USSR and the GDR. As usual, there were a few splendid vaults by isolated competitors such as Blagoeva from Bulgaria and the Czechs, Nemethova and Dörnakova, all of whom scored 9.30, but once the Soviets came to the horse we were in another gymnastic world altogether. The lowest of their six scored 9.20; Tourischeva (now 19) and the 18-year-old Lazakovitch made 9.60, Burda 9.50 and the unknown miniature reserve, Korbut, 9.45 – the four highest scores in the competition. The East Germans, Janz and Zuchold, were also on 9.45.

The pattern never changed. The USA

At medal time in Munich, Korbut's tears give way to the smiles that made her the world's favourite girl, but it is Karin Janz who reigns supreme on the bars

made a fine showing on the asymmetric bars. Hungary, led by the splendid Ilona Bekesi, totalled 47 points. The USSR put up 47.70, and the GDR 48.00, averaging 9.60 among their five scorers. Janz led the field with 9.85, Zuchold had 9.70, and both Tourischeva and Korbut 9.60.

The Soviet gymnasts went further ahead on the compulsory beam, with Lazakovitch recording 9.40, and on the floor they were simply superb. Again they recorded the top four scores of the competition: Tourischeva 9.80, Lazakovitch 9.70, Korbut 9.60 and Burda 9.50, equalled by Janz. At the end of the compulsory section, the USSR totalled 189.15 to the 187.30 of the GDR – both already virtually out of reach of Hungary, Czechoslovakia and the USA. Britain was last of the 19 teams at that stage, with Yvonne Mugridge's 8.65 on the floor the best mark, compensating for her vault score of 6.10.

There were three East Germans and three from the Soviet Union in the top six as the optionals began, headed by Lazakovitch, but all encompassed within 0.75

points. On the optional vaults, it was the story as before with minor variations. Janz pulled out a 9.80 and Zuchold a 9.70; Tourischeva and Korbut registered 9.70 and 9.60. The GDR took the optional bars too, where both Janz and Korbut scored 9.70, and Elaine Willett scored Britain's only 9.00; and three-quarters of the way through the team competition the USSR were still almost comfortably ahead with 284.35 to the 282.85 of the GDR. On the individual front, things were hotting up: Janz was in the lead with 57.65, followed by Tourischeva with 57.40, Korbut 57.20, Zuchold 57.10 and Lazakovitch down to 57.05.

By now the German team knew they had no hope, for nobody can catch the Soviet artists on the beam and the floor, particularly in the optional exercises. Their beam work was a dream, winning 9.75 for Tourischeva, Korbut and Lazakovitch and the immense team score of 48.20, and it took them more than three-and-a-half points clear. Tourischeva was now level with Janz, with Korbut 0.20 behind. But though there were only the floor exercises to come in the team classification, the leading thirty-six competitors would go through their programme again before the individual all-round winner would be decided – and there lay the popular tragedy of the week.

Sure enough the USSR strengthened their lead on the floor, Korbut scoring 9.75, and Tourischeva and Janz 9.70. The team medals went to the Soviet Union (380.50), the German Democratic Republic (376.55) and Hungary (368.25). At that point Janz and Tourischeva were still neck and neck for the individual title, on 76.85. Korbut was third with 76.70, and Lazakovitch fourth with 76.40 (from a possible 80

points). And so to the drama of Wednesday, the fourth day.

The thirty-six, who included the entire Soviet and East German teams, were to perform optional exercises in all events again, a possible 40 points, to be added to half their preliminary scores, i.e. 38.425 in the case of the two leaders. Erika Zuchold vaulted to 9.70, and Janz, Tourischeva and Korbut were all awarded 9.65: no change so far. The bars: Janz and Tourischeva each recorded the same score as their earlier optional – 9.70 for Janz and 9.65 for Tourischeva.

Korbut too had scored 9.70 last time, but disaster awaited her efforts now. She made a hash of her take-off, faltered in her first few swings, recovered to a dazzling conclusion, but was marked down to 7.50 – by far the lowest score of the individual final, and one from which she could not possibly reach the medals. While Tourischeva and Janz tied on the beam at 9.40, Korbut hit 9.80. She won 9.80 for the floor too, but Tourischeva was majestic: 9.90 against Janz's 9.70. Thus it was that Tourischeva was rightly crowned the queen while the world was looking at a tearful princess who finished in seventh place.

For what it is worth, had Korbut scored her expected 9.70 on the bars, she would have just pipped Janz to the silver medal (Lazakovitch took the bronze). However, the Olympic story is full of ifs and buts, and little Olga was not done yet. The individual events competition was to come, and the world – certainly the packed Munich hall – was willing her to great things there.

Only six competitors contest each event – the top six scorers after the compulsory and optional exercises during the team competition. Tourischeva, Janz and Korbut were in every final; Lazakovitch was out of the bars and Zuchold was out of the floor. Again, the finalists start each event with the average of their scores in it during the team competition. This had Tourischeva ahead of Janz and Zuchold in the vault, but the champion managed only 9.60 while Janz collected 9.90 and the gold, and Zuchold 9.70 for the silver.

On the bars Korbut was determined to redeem herself. Janz, the leader at the start, put on another brilliant performance for 9.90 again. Korbut, whose preliminary mark, remember, did not include the disastrous 7.50, went through a routine that seemed to many of the crowd every bit as good as that of Janz, but she received only 9.80. The anguished spectators, who had come to see their darling win gold even if it meant depriving a German of the honour, created a storm of abuse which they hurled at the judges. According to Christopher Brasher in his book *Munich 72*, 'for a full ten minutes they howled and whistled in derision'. The judges may have flinched, but they did not alter the score: another gold to Janz, silver to Korbut, bronze to Zuchold.

In *The Times*, John Hennessey wrote: 'The stadium was in an uproar after another dazzling performance on the asymmetric bars, to match the one she had given in the team competition on Tuesday. On Wednesday this exercise had been the instrument of her humiliation when she had missed her take-off and failed to find her rhythm. Now she was her impish, breathtaking self again and the spectators were so dissatisfied with her 9.80 marks, a splendid score in all conscience, that they demonstrated loud and long. Finally an East German girl, Angelika Hellmann, putting her finger to her smiling lips in a plea for silence, braved the storm and dissolved in tears when a fluffed landing ruined her performance.'

However scrupulous and statuesque the judges, they could hardly fail to have been affected by the incident, and it is not impossible that in the next event at least, the beam, they were a shade generous to Korbut. Certainly Lazakovitch, who began the beam 0.75 ahead of her young rival, could not conceal her surprise (and some called it disgust) when Korbut was awarded 9.90, and the gold medal, to her own 9.80. And though the serene and admirable Tourischeva did not show a flicker when precisely the same marks were awarded on the floor in precisely the same situation, she was entitled to her thoughts. So there it was: two golds and a silver to Korbut, two golds and a silver to Janz, but the gold they all wanted most to Tourischeva. Like ice skating, gymnastics (and particularly floor exercises) cannot be judged without emotion. Korbut, who retired from competitive gymnastics in 1977 and from the sport altogether in 1978, plucks like a harp-player at your emotional strings. Listen to Brasher: 'How do you describe enchantment? Anyone who has seen Olga in the flesh or on television knows that she has an indefinable quality – perhaps best described as abandonment to the joy of life – which entirely captures people's hearts.'

After all that, one turns to the men's competition with an inevitable sense of anticlimax. One knew from the start that Japan would be in complete control of the team competition, and indeed they had their biggest-ever win over the USSR – 571.25 points to 564.05. In Mexico they had four individuals in the first five, and three of them (Kato, Kenmotsu and Nakayama)

The almost-forgotten Soviet heroine, Tamara Lazakovitch, on her way to a silver medal on the beam. She won the bronze in the overall classification

were still in the team and were to win the gold, silver and bronze medals in Munich – the first time since 1900 that had happened. Andrianov of the USSR, who was to become Olympic champion in 1976, was in fourth place. Below him in the all-round final placings came one of the two new members of the Japanese team, Kasamatsu (who replaced former Olympic champion Yukio Endo). Tsukahara came eighth and Okamura eleventh – what a ridiculously overwhelming line-up!

Sawao Kato became only the third man in history to win the individual championship twice (following Braglia, of Italy, and Chukharin, of the USSR). At the end of the six compulsory exercises of the team competition, he led with 57.35 from Andrianov (57.30), Kenmotsu and Nakayama. Andrianov's stupendous all-round skill was underlined by his never scoring less than 9.50, but in the optionals he dropped to 56.50 while there were four Japanese with more than 57. They were headed by Kato again, and though his three rivals all bettered his total in the final run, he held on to his lead.

The individual apparatus events were nobody's pushover. Kato and Kenmotsu reached every final, but no gymnast won more than one of them. Kato took the parallel bars, Nakayama the rings and Tsukahara the high bar (in which the first five places were filled by Japanese). The floor exercises were won by Andrianov, the pommel horse by his compatriot Klimenko and the vault by an East German, Klaus Koeste. An admirable distribution of trophies, but there was no glory to spare for the English-speaking nations. The USA, with a full team, were most disappointed to finish only tenth. The British trio were placed 93rd, 103rd and 107th out of the 113 competitors.

In the British Olympic Association's official report on the Games, Jim Prestidge wrote of the gymnastic achievement: 'Our men and women were so near the bottom that excuses can only underline our deficiencies. Brave performances, without a doubt, but bravery is not enough ... Gymnastics begins in schools and that is where the remedy must also start.' But that is another story.

3 1976: Comaneci at Montreal

And so to Montreal, where the men's and women's team competition began on 18th July, 1976. Once again, the only doubt with the men was how closely the Soviet Union could push the Japanese – and the answer was, very closely indeed. At the end of the compulsory exercises, the USSR led by half a point, but Japan took the optionals by almost twice that margin. In the final team analysis, the Japanese domination of the parallel bars with three men in the first four, and the high bar, where they took the first four places, was the overwhelming factor in their fourth successive team win.

The exciting development of women's gymnastics in Romania since Munich, where they were sixth with a total team mark that was beaten by all twelve competing nations in 1976, meant that they had potentially to be reckoned, with the German Democratic Republic, as providing sufficient opposition to worry the Soviet women. Not quite enough, as it turned out, for at the end of the team contest, the superbly consistent Soviet gymnasts had all six women within the top eleven places. Romania's competitors were strung out twice as far and the East Germans even further. The outstanding Romanian event was the asymmetric bars, where they amassed the score of 98.50 out of 100 (remember that only the top five gymnasts of each team contribute to the score). The USSR won every other event, though they had little to spare on the beam, and were more than three points clear of Romania in the final tally.

However, the Olympic Games was always primarily a contest to find the greatest individual performer, and here the lips were licked in anticipation of some marvellous struggles. Unusually, the top four men from Munich were still in the hunt: Kato, Kenmotsu and Nakayama from Japan, and Andrianov of the USSR – their only survivor. Among the women, the Soviet Union could still produce Tourischeva, the reigning champion, Korbut and Saadi. The GDR had lost the great duo of Janz and Zuchold, but Hellmann was still there (sixth in Munich). However, there were at least three newcomers who had so excited all who had seen them in the previous two years that, in the minds of many observers, the women's individual competition was at its most open. The new stars of the sport were Nelli Kim of the USSR and the two Romanian nymphs, Teodora Ungureanu and – above all, even above Tourischeva and Korbut – the new European champion, 14-year-old Nadia Comaneci.

The first time an English-speaking nation had seen this little genius had been in April 1975, when she appeared at Wembley in the first Champions All tournament. Her work on the bars and the beam was something nobody who saw it could ever forget, and to them it was not surprising that she went on to take the European championship in Norway later that year, performing a superb Tsukuhara vault and her unique version of the Radochla somersault on the asymmetric bars. For her to repeat such a triumph, at such an age, in the agonisingly tense atmos-

If Munich belonged to Korbut, Montreal was
stormed by Comaneci. The 14-year-old Romanian,
here on the way to a bronze on the floor, won
three gold medals

Nadia Comaneci's perfect dismount from the bars
in the team competition. Each of her four
performances on the bars won her the unique
mark of 10 out of 10

phere of an Olympic gymnastic competition, the grand theatre of the Games, was
too much to expect. Come what may, however, she was going to demonstrate some
techniques that would astonish the world.

The team groupings at Montreal put
together the GDR, the USSR, Romania
and Hungary, to perform in the afternoon.
In the compulsories, Tourischeva and Kim
vaulted to a 9.80, Korbut to 9.75, Saadi to
9.70; Comaneci headed the Romanian
effort with 9.70. On the bars, Korbut was
at her spellbinding best: 9.90. There was
9.80 for Kim and 9.75 for Tourischeva –

how could you answer that sort of scoring?
Nobody but the Romanians could: 9.75 for
Trusca, 9.85 for Constantin, 9.90 for Ungureanu and the first of the unbelievables
– a perfect 10.00 for Comaneci, the first in
Olympic history. She led on the beam too,
with 9.90 to Korbut's 9.80, but on the floor
the queen, Tourischeva, reigned supreme
with 9.90. Kim and Grozdova both scored
9.80, Nadia 9.75. At the end of that first day
these were the leading scores: Comaneci
39.35, Tourischeva and Ungureanu 38.85,
Grozdova, Kim and Korbut 38.80.

On the afternoon of the second day, the

Comaneci returns to the top bar after her famous personal version of the Radochla somersault. Even to see it, said one reporter, is not to believe it

world's greatest female gymnasts took the stage again, for the optional exercises. The pattern was much as before: superb vaulting by the Soviets – 9.90 for Kim and the diminutive Filatova; 9.85 for Comaneci, 9.80 for Tourischeva. Now, the bars. Could Nadia possibly repeat such perfection? Korbut repeated her 9.90, Kim and Tourischeva both improved on their first round marks with 9.85 and 9.80. The challengers overwhelmed them: 9.85 for Trusca and Constantin, 9.90 for Ungureanu, another 10.00 for Comaneci. The excitement in the Forum was volcanic, as one became aware

that this little schoolgirl was drawing away from those we had long regarded as unbeatable.

She topped the scoring on the beam too, with her third perfect mark, and one was beginning to wonder by how great a margin she was going to win the gold medal. There were three 9.85 scores on the beam, for Ungureanu, Tourischeva and Korbut, and if nothing else, the battle for second place was going to be very close. Only the floor was to come, before the final round, and here the Soviet girls were sure to advance. They did: Tourischeva 9.95, Kim 9.90, Filatova and Comaneci 9.85.

With the first eight exercises over, and 80 the possible score, Comaneci was on 79.05. Kim and Tourischeva had 78.25,

It is on the beam that Nadia's genius can be most clearly seen, and the ecstatic crowd at Montreal saw her win the gold with three more 'perfect' marks

Ungureanu 78.05 and Korbut 77.95. As usual, those marks would be halved and added to the score obtained in a final round of voluntary exercises, to make a new 'possible' of 80. One compromise was in force this time: as usual, 36 competitors would contest the final round, but not more than three were allowed from any one nation. This rule eliminated such a brilliant gymnast as Elvira Saadi, who though she was then standing in seventh place, was the fourth Soviet competitor. It let in to the final round Britain's Avril Lennox from 53rd place and Monique Bolleboom of Holland, (62nd),

and maybe that was no bad thing, artificial though it may have been. In the individual classification at that stage, incidentally, Comaneci led the bars and the beam, Kim the vault and Tourischeva the floor.

So, after a day's break, to the combined exercises final round, with Kim and Tourischeva knowing they had to make up 0.45 on the Romanian to beat her to the gold – far from impossible over four exercises, but unlikely in view of the almost certain fact that Comaneci was going to go further ahead of them on the bars and the beam. The two Soviet girls made a brilliant start on the horse: Kim recorded a 10.00, the first perfect vault ever achieved, and the defending champion 9.95. Comaneci took 9.85, Korbut 9.80 and Ungureanu 9.75. Total now:

'She's done it again!' – a gorgeous shot of the Romanian team acclaiming the golden girl at the ringside: Constantin, Comaneci, Ungureanu and Gabor

Comaneci 49.375, Kim 49.125, Tourischeva 49.075.

The bars produced either the most tolerant judging or the most excellent performing ever seen in a major competition. The lowest mark among the 36 competitors was 9.10. Tourischeva scored 9.80 and it virtually killed her chances of catching the Romanian. There were 9.90 scores for Egervari (Hungary), Korbut, Ungureanu and Kim. Comaneci scored 10.00 again, her third successive perfect score on the bars. When she followed that with her second successive 'possible' on the beam, the gold medal was hers as long as she completed the floor exercises competently.

The fight for the silver and bronze was desperately tight. Tourischeva drew level with Kim by scoring 9.85 on the beam to 9.70, and the defending champion had her best exercise to come, the floor. Korbut, who had been only 0.20 behind, ruled herself out of the medals by what was for her a disastrous exercise on the beam, drawing 9.50. Ungureanu had made a great effort with another 9.90 on the beam and was then only 0.15 behind the two Soviet gymnasts. The floor settled it: for the first time in the competition, Kim outscored Tourischeva, 9.95 to 9.90. Ungureanu could not beat that (9.80) and Comaneci did not have to (9.90). Korbut kept herself comfortably in fifth place, and for most of the huge crowd remained the darling of the scene just the same. Beside her vivacity, Comaneci performs like a mechanical doll – but, of course, one whose perfection is breathtaking.

The Times reporter this year was Jim Railton, more of an expert on water than in the gym, but his summing-up of the day was accurate enough: 'Comaneci became the new superstar of women's gymnastics by winning the combined individual exercises with yet another series of perfect marks of 10 in the asymmetric bars and the beam. Her cool and professional presentation captured the crowd once more and led to a standing ovation.... While Olga Korbut,

The baby of the Soviet team was 4 foot 6 inches high (1.37 m) newcomer Maria Filatova. In ninth place after the team exercises, she was still only the fifth-placed Russian

although not the perfect gymnast in Munich, entranced a worldwide audience with her charm and gaiety, the mechanical precision of Comaneci took over here in every sense this afternoon.'

Like most reporters assigned at the Olympics to keep their eye on several events at once, Railton had been doing so through the great banks of television monitor screens provided for the Press at every

venue. He hurried over to the gymnastics, he said, when on those colour screens 'Nadia appeared as a bright blue extra-terrestial star, whereas Miss Tourischeva looked as if she was being throttled by her leotard.'

There were still four gold medals to decide, for the individual events. As ever, these are fought out between the six gymnasts with the highest scores in the two rounds, compulsory and voluntary, of the team competition. In each event, those totals are halved and added to one final voluntary exercise. Comaneci was the only gymnast to contest all four finals. Kim was not in the beam, Tourischeva not in the bars. Ungureanu and Korbut were only in the beam and bars, and the competitions included some of the rising names in the sport. Escher Gitta of the GDR, for instance, contested three finals and her compatriot Marion Kische, two. Carola Dombeck, also of the GDR, won the vaulting bronze, and Egervari the bronze on the bars.

The eyes of the vast public were, as usual, only for the stars. Though Comaneci went into the final round of the vault lying behind Kim and Tourischeva, she was edged out of the medals by Dombeck, who took 9.90 to tie on total score with Tourischeva. Kim, with 9.95, was well clear for the gold. Comaneci did what was by now expected of her on the bars: yet another 10.00, her fourth on that apparatus and her sixth of the Games. Team-mate Ungureanu, who scored 9.90 every time on the bars, won the silver, only 0.025 ahead of Egervari. Korbut, who came to this final with the same score as Ungureanu, hit her lowest mark of the Games: 9.40.

Both Korbut and Ungureanu took 9.90

Eighth in Munich, seventh in Montreal, fourth in the world championships, third in the World Cup: there are few 'also-rans' more talented than Elvira Saadi

The faces of the watchers tell the story: this vault by Nelli Kim in Montreal was the first in Olympic history to win perfect marks: 10 out of 10

on the beam, for silver and bronze, but Comaneci rang the bell again: her seventh mark of 10.00, giving her 19.95 out of 20. Kim continued her magnificent improvement on the floor, scoring 10.00 to Tourischeva's 9.90. A 9.95 for Comaneci kept her in third place, well clear of another fast-improving gymnast, Anna Pohludkova of Czechoslovakia. Thus ended the most sensational Olympic gymnastic competition ever held, with the thought reeling about the minds of most of us: can Comaneci, who in 1984 will be only 22 years old, become the first gymnast in history to take the all-round gold medal three times?

With the men's teams of Japan and the Soviet Union being so far ahead of their challengers, the GDR and Hungary, it was inevitable that the individual classification would be dominated once again by gymnasts from those two countries. At the end of the team competition, there were four from each of them in the top nine, with the supreme all-rounder, Andrianov, 0.60 ahead of Sawao Kato, the champion of both the Mexico and Munich Games. Andrianov's consistency is quite staggering. At that point he stood first on the rings, second on the vault and parallels, third on the floor and pommels, and tenth on the high bar (at which he had been second after the compulsories).

He moved inexorably towards his all-round gold medal in the final round, leading the scoring on the floor, rings and vault. Kato was not at his best, and ended a full

Nadia's friend and rival, Teodora Ungureanu, took the bronze medal on the beam at Montreal and missed the all-round bronze by only one quarter-point

Israel's only gymnast in Montreal, Dov Lupi, works on the parallel bars. He was the first male gymnast from his country ever to compete in the Olympics

point behind him, but still ahead of Tsuka-hara, Ditiatin and Kajiyama. Among the tragedies of that final round, which saw three men retire injured, perhaps the most unfortunate was that of Vladimir Markelov (USSR). At the end of the team competition he was lying fourth and well in the hunt for medals, but after completing four of the six events in the final round he had to pull out. So did poor Danut Grecu, of Romania, who soldiered on through injury to score only 3.00 on the floor and 0.40 on the pommels.

Andrianov took another three golds in the apparatus championships, on floor, rings and vault, as well as a silver on the parallel bars and a bronze on the pommel horse. Only his fellow-countryman Boris Shakh-lin, in 1960, has ever had a record to equal it. Kato, the runner-up, took the parallel bars gold and Tsukuhara the high bar, but it was good to see a couple of outsiders

among the medals. Zoltan Magyar, on the pommel horse, became the first Hungarian man to win a gold medal in gymnastics for 44 years, and with a bronze for his floor exercises Peter Kormann became the first American of either sex to win any gymnastic medal since 1932 – when the Games were held in Los Angeles.

It had been an altogether satisfying and exciting competition, won by one of the finest gymnasts the world has ever seen. Those of us not competent to rank with the judges in our understanding and appreciation of the sport were left with one puzzling thought: is the standard of women's gymnastics really so far ahead of men's that there should be only nine scores of 9.90 in the entire men's competition, while the women were awarded that and more every few minutes?

4 Biographies

ANDRIANOV, Nikolai (1953–): tremendous Soviet competitor who reached four of the six individual apparatus finals in the 1972 Olympics (Munich), winning the gold on the floor and the bronze on the vault, and in 1976 (Montreal) won the combined title by a full point as well as gold medals for floor, rings and vault, the silver on parallel bars and the bronze on the pommel horse.

Andrianov (USSR) seen here on the pommel horse won four gold medals at the Montreal Olympics in 1976

ASTAKHOVA, Polina (1936–): Ukrainian (USSR) gold medallist on the asymmetric bars in the Olympic Games of 1960 (Rome) and 1964 (Tokyo). In the same two Olympics won silver medals on the floor and bronze in the combined individual, as well as being a member of the winning USSR team in 1956–60–64. It was her misfortune to be a Soviet contemporary of the brilliant Latynina, and at the moment when that hurdle might have been overcome, to find Caslavska had arrived.

Former world and Olympic champion Vera Caslavska

Caslavska won 22 world, Olympic and European titles

BRAGLIA, Alberto (1883–1954): Italy's most celebrated gymnast, he won a gold medal for combined exercises in the interim Olympics of 1906 (Athens) and was the official Olympic all-round champion of 1908 (London) and 1912 (Stockholm), where Italy also won the team event. Became the national coach and held the position when Italy took the team and individual championships in 1932.

CASLAVSKA, Vera (1942–): perhaps the most glamorous figure in the history of women's gymnastics, the blonde Czech won seven Olympic gold medals and four silver, and between 1959 and 1968 took altogether 22 world, Olympic and European titles. In the early part of her international career she was consistently defeated by Latynina (USSR), and was 22 before winning her first Olympic medals in 1964 (Rome). There she won gold medals for beam and vault and beat Latynina by 0.03 for the combined individual title. She was world champion in 1966 and in Mexico in 1968 was the star of the Games, winning the all-round championship by a wide margin with the highest score ever recorded, taking gold medals for vault, bars and floor, and silver for beam. She then retired and married the Czech 1500 metres runner, Josef Odlozil, in Mexico City while the Games were still on.

CERAR, Miroslav: brilliant Yugoslav all-rounder who won 16 world, Olympic and European gold medals between 1961 and 1970. Probably the greatest horse performer in history: three times world and twice Olympic champion.

CHUKARIN, Viktor (1921–): leader of the superb Soviet gymnasts who shook the world when, in 1952 (Helsinki) they entered the Olympics for the first time and won the men's and women's individual and team championships. Chukarin was individual all-round gold medallist in 1952 and 1956 (Melbourne), only the second man in history to have won the title twice. His victory over Ono (Japan) at Melbourne was by five-hundredths of a point. In 1952 won golds on pommel and vault, silver on bars and rings, and in 1956 gold on bars and a bronze on pommel.

COMANECI, Nadia (1961–): astonishing Romanian girl who, at the age of 14, was seven times awarded the 'perfect' mark of ten at the 1976 Olympics (Montreal). She won gold medals for beam and bars and a bronze on the floor, and took the combined title by a clear margin – the youngest Olympic champion in history. She first won the European championship in 1975 and was the first gymnast in the world to per-

The youngest of them all, Romania's Nadia Comaneci

form a Radochla somersault on the higher of the asymmetric bars.

ENDO, Yukio (1937–): (Japan) overall Olympic champion in 1964 (Tokyo), where he first performed the extremely difficult stunt on the high bar that became known as an Endo. He won only one apparatus gold medal in his career (parallel bars, 1964), but took a bronze on the floor the same year, and a silver for the vault in 1968 (Mexico). The only member of all three winning Japanese teams in the 1960–64–68 Olympics.

GOROKHOVSKAYA, Maria: (USSR) the first female Olympic combined exercises individual gold medallist, at Helsinki (1952), where the USSR competed for the first time and won the team championship which they have never lost. Her achievement of winning the silver medal in every apparatus event is unique.

GRAVELET, Jean-Francois (1824–97): (France) world-famous as Blondin, the tightrope walker who first crossed the Niagara Falls in 1859, pushing a man in a wheelbarrow along the 1100-feet rope, 160 feet over the water.

JAHN, Johann (1778–1852): German enthusiast who created the parallel bars, the rings and the high bar, and has more right than any to be regarded as the founder of modern gymnastics. Started many gymnasia over the country and strove to establish strength as the predominant requirement, rather than subscribing to the free-flowing ideals of his Swedish contemporary, Ling.

KATO, Sawao (1946–): third man in the world to win the individual Olympic title twice – in 1968 (Mexico) and 1972 (Munich). Won the floor gold and rings bronze in 1968, and in 1972 gold on the parallel bars and silvers on high bar and pommel. In 1976 (Montreal) won the parallel bars and came second overall, giving him the finest male Olympic record in history. Japan won the team gold on all three occasions.

Nelli Kim (USSR), who twice scored 10 in Montreal

KIM, Nelli (1957–): outstanding Soviet gymnast who rose from obscurity in 1972 to become runner-up to Comaneci in the 1976 Olympics (Montreal). Was the only other competitor there to receive a 'perfect' ten, which she did in both floor and vault, both of which titles she won.

KORBUT, Olga (1955–): (USSR) probably the most famous gymnast in the world, despite never having won a major all-round title, nor a combined exercises Olympic medal of any kind. The projection of her elfin personality by television in the 1972 Olympics (Munich) made her the star of the Games, but though winning gold medals for floor and beam, and silver for asymmetric bars, she finished only seventh in the all-round individual classification.

LATYNINA, Larisa (1934–): (USSR) only one Olympic competitor (the standing jumper, Ewry, in 1900–04–08) has won more gold medals than this great Ukrainian performer, who altogether took 24 Olympic, world and European gold medals, despite giving birth to two children during her career. The supreme Olympic champion in 1956 (Melbourne) and 1960 (Rome),

Perhaps the greatest of them all, Larissa Latynina

she won the floor exercises for three successive Olympics and the vault in 1956. In 1958 she won five gold medals in the world championships. Her full Olympic record – 1956: combined gold, vault gold, floor gold, bars silver; 1960: combined silver, floor gold, bars silver, beam silver, vault bronze; 1964: combined silver, floor gold, vault silver, beam bronze, bars bronze. She remains the only gymnast in the world, of either sex, to have won medals in every event on the programme in two Olympics.

LENNOX, Avril (1956–): though insignificant by international standards (she was 53rd in the Montreal Olympics of 1976), the outstanding British gymnast of the decade. Won the national title four consecutive years before retiring, through injury, at 21 to take up coaching.

LEOTARD, Jean (1838–?): French gymnast and acrobat who invented the trapeze in 1859 and gave his name to the garment now worn by most female gymnasts and dancers.

LING, Per Henrik (1776–1839): creator of the system known as Swedish gymnastics, in which movement is rhythmic and fluent, and fixed apparatus has no part. Ling saw gymnastics as an integral part of education and not as a club activity.

MAGYAR, Zoltan (1953–): superb Hungarian pommel horse specialist, unbeaten in world, Olympic and European championships from 1973 to 1978.

NAKAYAMA, Akinori (1943–): one of the greatest gymnasts never to win the combined Olympic title, he was overall bronze medallist twice (1968 and 1972), in each case less than half a point behind the winner, his Japanese team-mate, Sawao Kato. Won the gold on the rings and the silver on the floor in both Games in 1968; also won the parallel bars and high bar.

ONO, Takashi (1931–): leader of the Japanese team that first wrested world and Olympic supremacy from the USSR, he was twice beaten for the Olympic all-round championship by only 0.05 points – in 1956 (Melbourne) by Chukarin and in 1960 (Rome) by Shakhlin. As well as those silver medals, won gold on the high bar in 1956 and 1960, and the vault in 1960; silver on the pommel in 1956; and bronze for vault

Nadia in 1975 with British champion Avril Lennox

in 1952 and parallel bars in 1956 and 1960. Won team gold medals in 1960 and 1964.

SCHWARZMANN, Alfred (1912–): remarkable not only for his 1936 Olympic achievement, when in his native Berlin he won gold medals for combined individual, team and vault; and bronze for high bar and parallel bars; but particularly for returning to the Olympic scene in 1952 (aged 40) and winning a silver on the high bar.

SHAKHLIN, Boris (1932–): extremely strong USSR gymnast whose only weakness was on the floor, he won the combined exercises Olympic gold in 1960 (Rome) and nine other Olympic and world gold medals. At Melbourne in the 1956 Olympics, a pommel and team gold; in 1960, pommel, vault and parallel bars gold, rings silver and high bar bronze; in 1964, high bar gold, team silver and rings bronze. In the 1958 world championships, he won five gold medals.

STALDER, Josef: Swiss gymnast whose name lives on with a popular and complicated stunt on the high bar. In the 1948 Olympics (London) he won the high bar gold medal and parallel bronze, and in 1952 (Helsinki) the combined bronze, high bar silver and parallel bronze. Switzerland were team silver medallists in both Games.

STUART, Nik: British national coach who had an astonishing domestic gymnastics career. He won the national championship for eight successive years, 1956–63, and even in his final year won all six events.

TOURISCHEVA, Ludmilla (1952–): classically correct Soviet gymnast who won the all-round Olympic title in 1972 (Munich) without winning a single individual event (she won a silver for floor and a bronze for vault). Out-gunned in popular appeal by her compatriot, Korbut, she suffered a similar fate

Tourischeva won every event in the 1975 World Cup

WORLD CUP
1975

Soviet double: Andrianov with Tourischeva

in Montreal (1976), where she worked in the shadow of the precocious Comaneci and won the bronze for combined exercises and the silver on floor and vault. World champion in 1970 and 1974, she followed Latynina and Caslavska in winning every gold medal in the 1973 European championships.

TSUKAHARA, Mitsuo (1948–): Japanese Olympic gymnast who in 1972 (Munich) won the gold medal on the high bar and the bronze on the rings, and in 1976 (Montreal) was third overall and won the high bar gold, the vault silver and the parallel bars bronze. Remembered for the vault bearing his name.

WALLENDA, Karl (1905–1978): founder and leader of the sensational high wire balancing act, the Great Wallendas. Created a seven-man pyramid in 1947. In 1962 the pyramid collapsed: two were killed, one paralysed. Another of the team was killed in 1963, and in 1978 Wallenda fell off a 120-foot wire in Puerto Rica when hit by a gust of wind.

YAMASHITA, Haruhiro: Japanese vaulter who won the event gold medal at the 1964 Olympics (Tokyo) with a vault never before seen in the Games, now a standard requirement for advanced competitors.

35

5 Tumbling

How very odd, to choose as the first example of gymnastic practice a section of the sport that is rarely seen and has no place in Olympic competition! The truth is that tumbling, the free movement of the body in acrobatic exercise, is the basis of much that is met elsewhere in the sport. Floor exercises are built on tumbling routines, men's consist of little else, they are an increasing ingredient of women's work on the beam, men use several of them on the parallel bars and trampolining is tumbling on springs.

Tumbling itself originated thousands of years ago, but has only recently become a world championship sport. Its championships used to be held in association with those of trampolining, but they are now officially embraced in the 'new' gymnastic excitements of sports acrobatics. Its history, recent development and competitive requirements appear later in the book. Here we are concerned not with the regulations of tumbling, nor with its integration into the Olympic floor exercises, but with some of its basic joyous movements – the only ones in the whole gymnastic programme that are unaided and unhampered by apparatus, and depend solely on the agility, skill and inventiveness of the gymnast.

That may be underselling it: a successful tumbler needs also to be exceptionally quick, flexible and well-coordinated, to have courage (as must all gymnasts) and strength. All in all, if you are a good tumbler, you are not likely to be a bad gymnast.

There is no obviously easy way in which to place the infinite variety of tumbling movements into compartments. Few stand on their own. They lead one to another, building into a fluent and complex routine in which it should be impossible to decide when the gymnast is ending one stunt and when he is beginning the next. We could begin by looking at those movements throughout which the performer remains in contact with the floor, and later go on to the more astonishing feats in which he (or she) becomes airborne.

Forward rolls

In one variety or another, probably the first and most natural tumbling movement anybody learns is the forward roll. Learning it from a static start, the gymnast will squat on the mat, hands well in front of feet, shoulders directly above hands. The movement springs from a vigorous straightening of the knees. The head is tucked between the arms and the body rolls forward on the shoulder blades. As the hips meet the mat, the performer gives the roll continued impetus by reaching forward and grasping the shins, holding the legs in their tightly tucked position until the upper body is upright and the weight securely on the feet.

A straddle roll is executed from a position in which the gymnast stands with his legs wide apart and straight and his hands on the mat. The wider apart the feet are the better, because it is not as easy to provide impetus from the straddle as from the squat. On take-off, he puts his hands behind his head, tucks it between his arms and his body ward to thrust the hands between the legs, so that they make contact before the feet. The trunk needs to continue its forward movement after the feet have reached the mat, and a firm push with the hands is necessary to bring the body up to the straddle stand again. With an almost exactly similar technique, a forward roll with straight legs can be accomplished. This time the hands reach forward in the roll outside the legs, not between them.

When those three movements have been perfected, the much more difficult dive roll can be tried. The performer needs two or three steps to run up, and the two-footed take-off must be high and strong. It is as if he were diving over a large barrel, so that the angle of descent is quite steep, with the body slightly piked – that is, bent at the hips, with the legs straight. As the hands hit the mat, the head is tucked well under and the forward roll proceeds as before. The momentum must be sufficient to bring the gymnast to his feet again.

Backward rolls

There is often a slight reluctance among beginners to try backward rolls, and a tendency to look over their shoulders to see what is happening behind them. From the squat stand, the gymnast must fall backwards, keeping the back well rounded by holding the head forward and hugging the knees. As the roll passes to the upper shoulder blades, he brings the hands forward to beside the head, pushing down to raise the body. The knees must be kept close to the chest until the feet are on the ground; the arms are now straight.

The back roll can be performed from a straddle stand just as the forward roll was. Again, the hands must be on the floor before the feet or the bottom. Once the seat is taking the weight, and the legs are rising, though still wide apart, the hands come beside the head, pushing strongly to raise the body. The legs come over the top, the feet return to the floor and the gymnast stands as he began.

Again, the roll can go backwards with straight legs as easily as it went forwards, with the hands outside the legs; and an impressive refinement can be added, when that is mastered, by pushing more quickly and more strongly with the arms as the legs reach the vertical, and at the same time stretching the body at the hips. Then, instead of completing the roll, the body can be halted in a handstand.

Headstand

Headstands and handstands can both be reached either by the usual kick-and-swing method, or through static strength. The latter is not for beginners, and indeed very young children do not have the muscular equipment to hold either position even though they have got there through swing. They must be assisted. The hands should be on the mat, shoulder width apart, any closer and the gymnast will lose stability. The head should be firmly between the hands, making contact just above the hair line. The idea is to spread the weight equally between the three points of ground contact, as, one leg at a time, the body swings up to a perfectly vertical position. When the muscles of the back and stomach are sufficiently developed, the legs can be brought up together and slowly.

Handstand

Children achieve handstands in the play-ground with an exaggerated swing, arching the body and raised arms backwards as one leg is lifted in front of them. The whole machinery is then rocked into position, probably against a wall, and why not? In the gym, however, tighter body discipline is required: one leg is thrust well forward, bent, and the arms fully extended above the shoulders so that they make a straight line with the body and the other leg. That line is maintained as it all tips forward. The hands are now on the floor, fingers wide-spread, the head still between the arms, and the rear leg pointing up at about 45 degrees. At the same time the forward leg extends firmly, sending the hips up. The straight line should be maintained, and the thrust-ing leg joins the other at the vertical. The head needs to be kept slightly back, looking at the fingers, to prevent the legs from con-tinuing their rotation. To return to the standing position, the legs should be fully split from the vertical, one going down at a time.

Later, the handstand can be reached by the slow strength method, and from any kind of standing position – squat, straddle, or straight legs. Once up, the legs may be split forwards and backwards, or straddled, or moved to the 'stag', a split in which one leg only is acutely bent at the knee.

Cartwheel

There is something very appealing about the joyful simplicity of a perfectly executed cartwheel. The entire body rotates side-ways, the limbs looking like spokes. The cartwheel must be learned in both direc-tions; when moving left the gymnast takes a step sideways on the left foot, places the left hand on the floor about a pace from the foot, and at the same time swings the right leg up high. As the movement continues, both hands are briefly on the floor, taking the body through a straddle handstand. The wheeling motion never stops, the arms must always be straight and the head held back. A good distance should be covered by the cartwheel, but it should not deviate from its line.

When a gymnast finds the regular cart-wheel comes as second nature, he may wish to try it using only one hand. This makes a shorter rotation, and it must be executed quickly. As we shall see shortly, top-class performers can do a cartwheel without using the hands at all.

Walkovers

The forward walkover is an extension of the handstand, continuing the rotation until the body is once more standing upright. As for the handstand, the legs come up one at a time, but the leading leg continues its move-ment over the head and beyond the vertical. Some coaches like the take-off leg to be 90 degrees behind the other, some like a full split to be seen before the leading foot comes to the floor. A variation of the walk-over sees the legs come together in the handstand position and limber over together to the floor. In either case, shoulder and back muscles must be very flexible.

So must they be for the backward walk-over, in which the body makes a bridge on its journey. Standing on one leg, with the other extended forward, the gymnast bends backwards till the hands reach the floor.

The leading leg by then is almost vertical, and continues to pass over the body, the other following well behind. As the gymnast regains his feet, the arms are held high.

Tinsica

A pretty movement, the tinsica is a cross between a forward walkover and a cartwheel. The gymnast steps forward with the take-off leg, holding one arm straight forward and the other above the head. The trunk bends, the take-off leg is placed firmly on the ground and the leading arm (the one on the same side as the take-off leg) follows it, a pace ahead. The swinging leg is by now high in the air behind the performer, and it remains a full stride ahead of the other. The second hand reaches the ground well ahead of the first, the body continues to rotate smoothly and the movement ends as it began – one leg forward, one arm forward.

That ends our rather arbitrary division of tumbling movements. These are the basic ground contact movements of the business, broadly outlined. Nor have we gone into any detail about the progressions and interweaving that the gymnast and his coach will soon be devising: the handstand that drops into a bridge and up again to a handstand, the backward roll that rises to a handstand and the forward walkover on one arm. One of the most fascinating aspects of gymnastics, tumbling in particular, is discovering where you can go from here. But it is time to look at springs and somersaults.

Round-off

You are not likely to see any demonstration of tumbling that does not include a round-off. It is one of the standard tricks for chang-ing direction on the move, often taking the gymnast from a forward run to a backward somersault. He takes off on one leg, arms extended above his head, aiming for a handstand. But, as in a cartwheel, one hand makes contact with the floor before the other, and about a step ahead of the take-off leg. The second hand is so placed that the shoulders execute at least a quarter turn while the take-off leg is catching up with its mate. The remainder of the 180-degree turn must be accomplished as the body passes the handstand, at which point the legs are snapped down towards the floor and the arms push sharply away. In a bent position, the body rotates rapidly until the performer is standing again, facing the opposite direction to that in which he started and ready to continue with a backward somersault or back handspring. The speed with which the round-off must be completed in order to provide the power for the next movement may cause the gymnast, in practice, to fall backwards when he tries to stop at the end of the round-off.

Headsprings and necksprings

Though you will see these performed by quite young children in a school gymnasium, it is not until the performer is a good deal more advanced that there is much flight to the spring. To achieve that requires considerable strength and application to technique. Both springs are executed in almost exactly the same way: from a standing position the gymnast leans forward and puts his hands on the mat, arms bent. For the headspring, the head is placed slightly in front of the hands, so that the three supports form a triangle. The legs are pushed off the ground almost before the head is down (it is the forehead that makes contact), and the head does not actually take any weight until the hips are rising towards the vertical. As the hips pass the vertical, the body straightens quite sharply and at the same time the hands push off strongly. The body takes an arched flight, arms held overhead, and there is an upright landing.

The obvious difference with the neckspring, or neck kip and head kip as they are sometimes known, is that as the head comes to the mat it is tucked under, between the arms. There needs to be considerably more force to the push off and to the simultaneous straightening of the body to bring the movement to a crisp conclusion.

Handspring

If the handspring is not to be merely a handstand into a bridge and stand, a great deal of work has to be put into the take-off. In the words of Akitomo Kaneko in *Olympic Gymnastics*, 'Many beginners fail to take it seriously enough, and then wonder why they cannot perform this stunt well.' Handsprings begin with a run and a strong hop, taking the body into the air as a preparation to take-off. This occurs in the same position as from a handstand, with the take-off leg well in front of the other, the body leaning forward and the arms up by the head – but of course all that is within one lively, running movement.

The straightening of the take-off leg should be really forceful, and so must the upswing of the trailing leg. Because of the speed of the whole movement, the hands will be on the floor for a very short time. The push-off must therefore be expertly timed, and must be made by coordinating arm and shoulder muscles. On landing,

knees and hips must be prepared to absorb the shock, otherwise the upper body will probably pitch forward; but more often than not, the expert will follow his handspring with another and another and then a forward somersault, and in such cases the landing is made on one leg.

From a back handspring, also known as a back flip or a flic-flac, there can be no running take-off. The impulsion comes solely from the thrust of the legs and the swing of the arms, and both must be powerful. Before take-off, the gymnast 'sits down' on air, keeping his head forward and his back straight. The arms are extended backwards and as high as possible at the beginning of the move, and swing strongly down and forward as the seat reaches its lowest position, the thighs parallel to the mat. As the arms continue their vigorous path upward, the feet thrust down into the mat to launch the body into its arched flight, led by the arms at full stretch. This is another very fast movement, and the body fairly whizzes through the handstand position, allowing very little time indeed for the push-off – which again should be made through the shoulders, with the arms locked straight. As soon as the legs pass the vertical, they snap down together towards the floor as the hands leave it, and the body returns to a standing position.

Somersaults

A marvellous sight, a somersault or two, and beloved of all tumblers. Learn it tucked first, because rotation is easier that way. Advanced gymnasts perform it also with bent or L-shape body and straight body. For 360-degree revolve in the air, the somersault or salto needs a running start and a two-footed take-off, at which point the arms, which have been forward, swing fully backwards. This helps both to lift the body and to produce rotation. In the air, the head bends down towards the stomach, the knees rise and the hands grasp the back of the thighs, helping to pull it into a tight tuck. The smaller it is, the faster it will turn. As soon as the head comes to the top again, the body is opened out for landing.

A back somersault, starting from a standing position, calls for explosive arm and leg action. As for the back handspring, the gymnast needs to lower himself to a crouch, arms extended behind him. Instantly, the legs thrust straight and the arms swing forward and upward. As soon as the feet leave the floor, he brings his knees up towards his chest and clasps them as he rotates backwards. He stretches his body for landing as soon as he faces the floor. It is worth noting that, in his book, Akitomo Kaneko warns that incorrect execution of the back somersault, usually at take-off, causes more Achilles tendon injuries than any other movement in the whole of gymnastics.

Free wheels

The free (or aerial) walkover and cartwheel are both difficult and complicated movements that must not be attempted without supervision. They require extraordinary flexibility of the back and hips, perfect technique and precise awareness of the body's characteristics while travelling through the air. Probably because of the purely physical requirements of these moves, they are more often performed by women than men. The operation must be accomplished with explosive speed; two or three free walk-overs would be completed while you are reading this one sentence.

The actual walkover take-off is preceded by a short run and one hurdle step. The weight comes down first on the rear (swinging) leg, then on the take-off leg; instantly the upper body swings down, the arms and the leg swing back and up, and the take-off leg thrusts straight – and all of that happens at once and with urgent power. There is no attempt in the free walkover to achieve distance. In flight, the body should be fully arched, and the landing should be as close as possible to the take-off. Unless all the movements are fast and vigorous, it is likely that there will not be enough rotating power to bring the body upright after landing.

The free cartwheel is similarly tackled, though there are basic differences in execution. The body is never arched, but remains straight throughout the flight, the head pointing to the floor. The legs too are stretched and all the time cover as wide a stride as possible. The swing up of the arms and legs needs to be equally vigorous. The landing is made initially on the swing leg, while the take-off leg is still in the air; the movement ends with a step back by the take-off leg, and the gymnast facing the direction from which he has come.

In the preceding pages, we have only just touched on the basic armoury of the tumbler – and that is to say, of the gymnast. From there, with experience and expertise, he begins to put together the spellbinding moves: somersaults with triple twist, round-off back handsprings, a round-off to a twisting swan dive – there is no end to them. In.the chapters that follow, we shall see how some of those basic moves are put to use in the Olympic exercises.

6 Floor Exercises

Today it would be almost impossible for hundreds of millions of spectators across the world to think of gymnastics without thinking almost immediately of the floor exercises. They seem to represent all that is most appealing, most sublime about the sport, and when the women take the floor the international popularity of gymnastics hits a phenomenal peak unknown at any other sporting moment except the World Cup soccer final. Strange to recall, then, that as far as Olympic competition is concerned the floor exercises are, by thirty-six years, the youngest of all events: they first entered the programme for the 1932 Games in Los Angeles.

It is not hard to see the reason for this extraordinary success. The floor provides the largest and the clearest arena of the entire competition; the event is by some way the longest in the programme, and at the same time the fastest-moving; it is the most natural of all exercises, and the most graceful; and gives the competitor the chance to demonstrate strength, skill, stamina, the utmost agility and his own personality. However, for all its all-round spectator appeal, it is seldom a reliable pointer to the supreme gymnast: only two women, Latynina and Caslavska, and two men, Kato and Andrianov, have ever won both the floor and the individual combined Olympic titles.

This is the only event in which both men and women have precisely the same equipment to work on: a mat the competing area of which is 12 metres square, and which

A 15-year-old in the Korbut tradition, Maria Filatova, won an ecstatic ovation for her floor work in Montreal and in 1977 walked off with the World Cup

in international competition is usually a plywood and sponge sandwich. There is, however, a considerable difference between the sexes in the way in which they execute the exercise. A woman must occupy the floor for between 60 and 90 seconds, compared to a man's 50 to 70 seconds, but is usually set fewer compulsory movements to pack into that time. A woman therefore has far greater opportunity for self-expression; because her exercise is performed to a musical accompaniment, the voluntary elements tend to be largely balletic, twinkling movements of grace, artistry and suppleness that display her relaxation and inventiveness. Most male gymnasts are less well-equipped by either nature or physique for such balletic displays, and both their compulsory and optional movements lay greater stress on sheer agility, supported by strength and balance. They should, nevertheless, demonstrate an harmonious and rhythmic unity in their work on the floor. It has long been a disappointing facet of men's floor work, at all but the very highest level, that they tend to present a succession of superb stunts, with too little skill, and perhaps thought, given to linking them with artistic fluency.

To step beyond either boundary of the time limits imposed in competition causes the judges to penalize the performance – less of a hazard to women, working to a set piece of music, as it may be to men. Men also have the greater tendency to overstep the physical boundaries of the mat, allowing an over-energetic agility movement to throw them off-balance. This too brings a points deduction, and is a particularly tricky hazard because judges want you to use as much of the mat as possible – sides and diagonals. A failure to do that also loses points,

as does an excessively long run into a stunt.

With the excellence of the acrobatics, the judges look for technical perfection of all basic movements, for complete coordina-

There is no other event that encourages such free expression of personality. It can lavishly and cleverly be used to mask any number of deficiencies

43

ABOVE: Heading the East German assault on Soviet gymnastic supremacy for many years was Karin Janz, European champion in 1969 and a medal-winner in two Olympics

LEFT: Another of the brilliant performers from the GDR, Angelika Hellmann, in an almost perfect balletic extension on the floor, all muscles in full stretch

RIGHT: Ludmilla Tourischeva, twice world floor champion and twice Olympic runner-up, superbly demonstrating what is meant by amplitude – doing nothing by halves

tion, certainty of balance, a proof of suppleness (of women in particular) and of strength (of men in particular), and for that favourite, mysterious gymnastic word, amplitude. As far as anybody knows, that means all movements must be complete, rounded, fully-expressed. A leg that should be stretched must be stretched to the full, there must be real spring in a leap, an unmistakable arch when an arch is required.

Choosing the right music is an art in itself for the female gymnast, and one which, at

Munich's Olympic floor champion, Olga Korbut, held by the camera in the middle of a splendid splits leap. But who knows whether she is coming or going?

its finest, makes as great a contribution to the complete performance as it can do in ice skating. Probably nobody who saw Vera Caslavska win the floor exercises at the 1968 Olympics will forget her interpretation of the *Mexican Hat Dance*. She was inspired by the music, and between them they overwhelmed the audience. To equally good effect in later years the 'gamine' performances of Olga Korbut and Nadia Comaneci made superb use of musical detail. The music is more than a background accompaniment; it is an active partner, chosen for a variety of qualities. Ideally, it should, as a whole, be a memorable and to some degree a captivating piece; it should adequately express the whole flavour of the exercise and of the gymnast's personality; and it should contain a sufficiently wide range of mood and timing to enable the performer to demonstrate her full repertoire. As if those strictures were not hard enough to meet, there are three technical requirements: the music must be played on one instrument only, must not be too loud and must come to a logical conclusion at the end of the exer-

It was always one of the great joys of watching Olga on the floor that she was capable of capturing her audience even with the simplest free movements

To see her running was to experience again the joy of uninhibited childhood, and she elevated to a movement of magic the matter of standing on one leg

cise. And that, of course, is between 60 and 90 seconds after it began.

Inevitably, the gymnast who is trying to put together a competition routine – and one that she will probably adhere to for two or three years, if it is successful – needs professional help with her music. Perhaps she finds an item that instinctively she feels is right for her, to which she really enjoys working. It has to be put in shape, cut down

to size, arranged for one instrument, if it is written for orchestra, and recorded. Not only must it reach its conclusion within 90 seconds, but it must open with a chord or a few notes that will enable the performer to pick up her active cue instantly. And she must get to know it so well that when she does have a mishap on the mat, she can unhesitatingly put her routine right back in line with the music – for the chances of

Perhaps he did finish his somersault in time, but he doesn't look as if he thinks he is going to, and there is little to suggest that he might be wrong

being accompanied live by the musician are remote. Almost certainly, the gymnast will carry her pre-recorded cassette about with her and hand it to the organizers wherever she competes. Make no mistake, the choice and the organization of music is worth a great deal of thought – and how lucky the girls are to be allowed to use it!

Some basic ballet movements now play a vital part in the training of young female gymnasts, and this has done much to enhance the performance particularly of the floor exercise. Ballet training strengthens the legs and refines their movement, but perhaps most importantly it teaches the gymnast how best to convey visually the mood of the music. Among the most talented of even the very young gymnasts

now, there are few untidy arm movements. They are extraordinarily graceful, both on the beam and on the floor. The arms, the wrists, the hands, even the fingers as well as the whole inclination of the body are all being used with economy, with beauty and with meaning. It is no surprise to learn that youngsters working seriously at the sport are now spending at least an hour a week purely on ballet.

Men do not play the thistledown game of acrobatic elfs and fairies into which the women's floor exercises have developed. At the advanced level, male gymnasts, like male swimmers, are much older than their female counterparts. They are physically fully developed – and need to be, for despite the fact that agility and swing count for more than strength over the whole of their gymnastic scene, it is still not possible to be an outstanding all-round gymnast without being well-muscled. The needs of the rings alone see to that, and even on the floor the judges expect to see two demonstrations of strength and balance that will be held for two seconds. As these static stunts did not figure in the tumbling section, now is the time to look at some of them in detail.

Scales

These are the feats in which the gymnast stands on one leg and extends the other and his trunk in various directions, holding them absolutely rock steady. You are not likely to see a man's floor exercise without one. In the front scale, the performer leans forward till his trunk is horizontal, holding his head back and keeping a slight arch in the lower back. The free leg is raised behind him as high as possible – at least to the horizontal – and the foot pointed. Arms are usually extended sideways or forwards.

Olga Korbut brought gymnastics to the world in 1972

Despite the enthusiasm for the sport in Britain, the nation still lacks a gymnast of international standing. This is former champion Tommy Wilson

Slightly less stable is the side scale, for reasons that become obvious as soon as you try it. The trunk tips sideways, the chest squarely facing front and the head kept back. It must tip at least as low as the horizontal, otherwise the free leg, which rises in the opposite direction, will not keep its necessary mark above the horizontal. A large mirror is very helpful to the gymnast in practising this and any other scale.

Perhaps the most impressive of the traditional scales is the one known as the Y-scale, because that is what it looks like. The free leg is again raised sideways and as high as possible, so that the hand on that side can be extended to grasp the ankle. Counterbalance is provided by the opposite arm, and by the fact that the trunk inevitably inclines off the vertical. It is important in the Y-scale that the performer resists the temptation to pull the free leg in front of him. It must be kept back, in the same plane as the rest of the body. The head must be held up, and the gymnast who can perform this scale without a grimace of discomfort

Nadia Comaneci, the first 'perfect' Olympic gymnast

1 Floor exercises: back flip

2 Floor exercises: tinsica

3 Floor exercises: forward somersault

is worth a medal, because extraordinary flexibility of the hips is needed.

Support seats

A variety of hand balances requiring considerable strength: the upper body remains upright, the arms locked straight and the fingers spread, with the hands on the floor pointing in the direction the gymnast is facing. In an L-support seat the legs are together and parallel to the ground; in V-support, they are together and as nearly vertical as the performer can get them, with his head back and his back rounded. For straddle support, the legs are spread wide and the hands are on the floor between them.

A more difficult variant to the support seats is the lever, in which the whole body is parallel to the ground. The arms may be straight or, in elbow levers, bent.

Handstands

Basic swung handstands were discussed in the previous chapter, but during their floor exercise men often demonstrate 'muscle-up' or 'press' handstands. These are achieved without any leg take-off, solely by slowly raising them under muscle power. The handstand may be reached from a variety of starting positions – indeed, given the necessary strength, they are almost limitless. Beginners usually start from a squat, positioning the body as though they were about to go into a forward roll. The hips are then lifted as soon as possible to the vertical, giving the body stability before the straightening of the legs at the hips begins. The legs can be brought up in the straddle, and only closed when the movement is completed. Somewhat more strength is needed to perform a press handstand from a straddle stand, and very much more, as well as greater flexibility, to achieve one with the legs completely straight.

A one-armed handstand is an unfailing delight and points winner, whether with legs straddled or together, but there is no handstand that raises greater admiration than that which begins in the most unlikely position: with the gymnast flat out, face down on the floor. Defying all human probability, he raises his body off the ground in a perfect horizontal line by arm and hand pressure under the point of balance. In measured, unhesitating progress, the hips continue to rise and the body levers majestically to a full handstand.

7 Vaulting

It happens that the writer was one of the worst vaulters who ever lived, apparently being constitutionally incapable of arriving on the springboard with both feet at the same time. This led to many humiliating and positively painful sessions in the school gym, where whichever way the short horse was turned this lad was unable to get his bottom over it or his feet on it. Attempts to remain permanently at the back of the queue for vaulting were expertly thwarted by one Sergeant Usher, a demon of the Army Physical Training Corps before he became the terror of all physically incompetent scholars. We regularly provided his light relief, and that of our more agile classmates, when he searched the waiting line with: 'Where is 'e, where is 'e? Come on out 'ere and give us a demonstration of your brilliance. Go on, run at it, run as if you meant it! Oh my Gawd, look at 'im! That 'orse is for you to jump over. Not through, not underneath, but over. Don't you understand that? Eh? Don't you? You've got two legs, 'aven't you, same as everybody else?'.

Few have such a lousy time of it as that. Vaulting is essentially the simplest, as well as the briefest, of all competitive gymnastic exercises, and it probably attracts more people into the sport than any other. Even among the world's great performers, there are remarkably few variations of vault, and it is unfortunate that the very simplicity of the exercise leads many gymnasts, even dedicated and comparatively polished ones, to suppose that there is no need to waste time practising their vaults – certainly not

The final phase of a handspring vault, in which the gymnast has allowed his left arm to drift out. This will almost certainly lead to a twisted post-flight

This vaulter has probably approached the horse at 15 mph and hit it with a pressure of 500 lb per square inch (100 kg per sq cm). Now he leaves on the postflight

Despite their importance to its history, the men of Sweden have made little impact on the sport since the war. Bo Stroenberg reaches for the horse's neck

until a day or two before competition when they devote a few minutes to brushing them up. What a desperate mistake! If you are interested in competing, at whatever level, remember that the vault is worth ten points – no less than any other event. If it seems to you a simple matter, then it should be a simple matter for you to perfect it. No doubt you will note, as you prepare to do so, that only one competitor in Olympic history, Nelli Kim in 1976, has executed what the judges regarded as a perfect vault – though those who remember the incredible Czech, Vera Caslavska, in Mexico may

wonder how much better a vault could be.

The piece of equipment you vault over in a gym is always called a 'horse', whether or not it has legs. Its origin is indeed a horse – a dummy horse made of wood on which Roman soldiers 2,000 years ago learned to mount and dismount. Warriors continued to train on such an item for centuries, certainly through the long years when a knight in heavy armour had to struggle onto the back of an enormous steed. Even when the 'horse' was first used in sport, early in the 19th century, it was much more for jumping onto than jumping over, and only a few

steps of run-up were allowed. Now, far greater interest is shown in how the gymnast gets off the horse than how he gets on it, but in men's vaulting in particular the old associations are firmly preserved.

Women vault over a broad horse in, as it were, the side-saddle position; men leap the long, narrow way, and that part nearest to them as they run up is called the croup, which is the rump of a live horse, and the furthest part is known as the neck. It used to be common to find vaulting horses a hundred years ago with a face painted on one end and a tail on the other. Long horse vaulters must not place their hands on the middle section, which is where the saddle would be; indeed, in another piece of male gymnastic equipment the 'saddle' is still represented: the pommel horse, or side horse as some know it, has two strong handles where the pommels, or peaks, would be at either end of a real saddle.

Whichever way you are vaulting over the horse, the basic mechanics are the same. Every vault has a primary phase that includes the run-up, the take-off from a sprung board, the flight in the air towards the horse and the positioning of the hands and body as the horse is touched; and a secondary phase, comprising the push-off, the flight from the horse and the landing.

You will hear these airborne journeys referred to as first flight and second flight, or preflight and postflight, or preflight and afterflight, depending who you are with at the time. Though the attention of spectators is usually focussed on the second flight, where most of the impressive stunts are placed, the judges are just as interested in the earlier one.

Officially, they are not interested in the run-up, though no doubt they cannot fail to be impressed by a good one. For the gymnast, there cannot be a more important part of the vault than this, its overture, which is so easy the beginner often fails to concentrate on it. An inconsistent run-up, lacking speed and determination and precision, is by far the most common fault seen in novice vaulting. Its results are obvious even to the

World vaulting champion in 1974, Olga Korbut shows a perfect line as she comes off the broad horse in a handspring. Note the bare feet and bandaged ankle

For a girl to achieve enough height off the horse for a tucked somersault, she must hit the springboard very hard. As ever, the run-up holds the key

unskilled eye: a take-off that does not provide sufficient height, a preflight that brings the body to the horse at the wrong angle, a push-off miserably incapable of powering the postflight, a badly-angled landing, a stumble, a fall. All of which the coach can trace to those first hesitant steps 20 yards (20 m) back.

The British national men's coach, Nik Stuart, likens it to the long jump: a gathering of your reserves of power, he says, to cram into one brief, dynamic movement. Meg Warren, the senior women's coach in Britain, believes firmly that no girl can be a good vaulter if she is not a fast runner, and she advises all young hopefuls to work on their running, really work on it, before they ever move on to actual vaulting. There are no marks awarded for a perfect run-up, but within a second or two you will lose plenty if you do not have one.

Like a long jumper's run, or like that of a pole vaulter, it must be absolutely consistent. Even at the end of her career, and even for routine practice, the British national champion Avril Lennox always got out the tape measure before she began vaulting. Every run-up was of precisely the same length, every foot fell each time on the same spot. In official competition, the length of a female run-up is unlimited, but males are restricted to $65\frac{1}{2}$ feet (20 metres). Nik Stuart recommends 45 feet (13.7 m) as the minimum in which the gymnast can achieve top speed, and that should be followed by three yards of 'coasting' in which you should stop pushing and 'float' before your final effort off the springboard.

The world-class vaulter may reach an approach speed as high as 25 feet (7.6 m) per second or 17 miles (27.35 km) an hour, and is then likely to exert a pressure on the springboard of between 700 and 1,000 pounds (319–454 kg) per square centimetre. The beginner intent on getting over the horse with the lowest possible straddle will neither need this speed nor be able to achieve it, but even the simplest vault

At this level of gymnastics, the horse is no longer just an obstacle to be cleared. It is the launching pad for an adventure in space, for a daring flight

The steeper the angle of descent to the horse in the preflight, the more certain the gymnast will go on turning over and cannot reverse the vault rotation

should be preceded by a run of maximum efficiency and relaxation. This is the only gymnastic event in which running is of any consequence (also the only one in which the prime part is played by the legs and hips), which probably accounts for the average gymnast paying so little attention to running style; but you only have to watch the superb running of Nelli Kim or Nikolai Andrianov to know it will be followed by a beautiful vault. The run is electrifyingly

4 Vaulting: Tsukahara vault

5 Vaulting: Yamashita vault

One of the leaders of the 'new' batch of gymnasts from East Germany, Kerstin Gerschau (ninth in the Montreal Games) showing how a body twists in flight

fast, and yet seems effortless; it is smooth, graceful and totally predictable; the feet are perfectly aligned, the carriage of the body does not deviate an inch, the arm action is controlled and regular. You are watching the perfect operation of a perfect machine – the human body in top gear and yet under control.

Unlike the track sprinter, whose speed at the end of his run may possibly be so great he cannot completely control his body, the vaulter must, like the pole vaulter, remain in absolute control. He has something most precise to do at the end of his run: one foot must strike a pre-determined spot to drive the body up the slope of the springboard. That last stride, at the end of which both feet hit the board together, the toes about 12 inches (30.4 cm) from the far end, is called the hurdle. You can see that the action is faintly similar to hurdling, though no effort of pushing the body up into the air is needed. The springboard is roughly two feet wide and four feet long, and slopes up to a height of 5 inches (12 cm) at the take-off spot. The vaulter may place it where it suits him best – the further the board is from the horse, the higher and, obviously, the longer, the preflight is likely to be.

Ideally, he hits the board at its most flexible point, landing on his toes, rocking to the balls of his feet and taking off again before his heels touch the board. In practice, the pressure with which he lands on the board is so immense he is unlikely to be able to keep his heels up. At the instant of impact, the knees are very slightly bent and the body is usually leaning back a shade. In the tenth of a second in which a gymnast remains on the board, the knees straighten rapidly and the body becomes vertical. The faster this happens, the better the preflight is likely to be.

What happens to the arms during the hurdle and take-off? They are obviously not needed to pump any more, so does it really matter what you do with them? In every athletic activity, and particularly in any activity in which the body moves freely through the air, correct positioning and re-action of the arms is immensely valuable. Experienced gymnasts do not have to think about their arms in vaulting, but watch

Tourischeva on her way to her second overall world championship in 1974, watched by the Soviet coach, legendary Latynina, herself twice world champion

them and you will see how well they are used. In the last two or three steps before the hurdle (that part of the run-up where Nik Stuart says you should be 'floating') the arms no longer work as pistons, but move down and back behind the body ready for a vigorous forward swing as the feet land on the board. Forward and upward they go, leading the body and a positive influence on the direction it takes.

Just what that direction needs to be, de-pends on the kind of vault being executed. Andrianov's preflight is likely to be so long he looks like a racing diver at the Olympic pool; a first-year schoolgirl is going to have the board not much more than an arm's length from the horse and her little bounce on to it will be with a bent body. Both of them know that the hands must get there first, to act as the pivot point over which the body rotates as necessary, and to provide such lift as is needed for the postflight. With the beginner, there will not be much rotation or much lift: she is merely passing over the horse in her simple straddle vault (legs spread outside arms) and is interested only in clearing it and landing safely on the other side. The Olympic gymnast has only just begun his vault when he reaches the horse: for him, the horse is not the first step in his descent, but a take-off platform for a dazzling postflight in which he may be twisting, somersaulting, piking or performing some combination of all three.

He will have hit the horse with a pressure of between 500 and 700 pounds (226–317 kg) per square centimetre, and will be immediately executing a fast and forceful push-off. The power cannot come from the arms, because the elbows must be locked and straight; the force is only from the hands, wrists and shoulders, which is why the success of the postflight depends so heavily on the height of the preflight, which is determined by the vigour of the take-off, which is achieved only through the speed and accuracy of the run-up. Back to square one! The advanced gymnast will arrive at the horse with a body that is either straight or slightly arched, head between the arms. The angle at which he meets the horse (and this applies to female competitors on the broad horse as much as to males on the long horse) depends largely on whether the second phase of the vault calls for forward or reverse rotation of the body. All vaults need one or the other.

Consider that simple straddle vault again, in which all you need to do is to put your hands on the horse, shoulder width apart, spread your legs wide and flick yourself over. The preflight of the novice will be so brief that the legs will rise to the straddle position straight from the springboard; a bent-body preflight, with the upper half leaning towards the horse too. But if that same vault is performed by a more experienced gymnast, who positions the board further away from the horse, there is room for the body to be fully extended, horizontally, in the preflight. Immediately the vault begins to look more graceful and more exciting, and immediately the gymnast needs to plan the angle at which he will approach the horse. Ideally, a line from feet to shoulders should extend to meet the horizontal at between 30 degrees and 45 degrees. Any less and it would not be rated a good or graceful vault; any greater and he would be in physical trouble.

The hands, as they hit the horse, block any further forward movement. The energy of the preflight, plus the power given by the push-off, must tip the body one way or the other. To achieve her straddle, the performer needs to raise the upper half of the body, rotating it around the hips so that she is more or less sitting up and facing forward as her body passes over the horse. This is known as a reverse-directional vault – rather perversely, you may think, since the gymnast is facing front. But if you demonstrate it for yourself with a pencil or a ruler in the air, you will see why. The natural rotation the body has begun to take as it dives towards the horse has been halted and reversed, and this can only be done if the angle of approach is relatively low. A higher preflight, and a steeper dive to the horse, cannot be reversed. The push-off then sends the gymnast into some form of handspring vault, in which the feet continue their forward rotation and the head follows where the feet have been. Forward-directional vaults are much the more popular among advanced performers (the Yamashita and Tsukahara are outstanding examples in competition), and they sometimes have to be bullied to work on reverses

like the stoop vault or the spectacular Hecht.

It is clear that the postflight changes radically from vault to vault. Ideally, the higher and longer the better, though obviously such a flight can only be achieved with

It is a view you may not recognize, but that is Olga Korbut going over the top and into a tucked somersault, or possibly two, to judge from her height

LEFT: A slender waif turns expertly into a Tsukahara. The right hand is ready to complete the twist, which will be followed by a one-and-a-half somersault

63

6 Vaulting: Giant Hecht

an advanced vault. All postflights should be clean and controlled, and in the women's side of the sport preflight and postflight should be of approximately equal length. One of the gymnast's most difficult problems is to land securely after a vault. The more experienced the performer, the more difficult this is, because the height and speed of the postflight is likely to increase. The body should be fully extended before landing, and the tendency to pitch forward counteracted by leaning back, short of the vertical, on contact with the mat, and slightly bending the knees to cushion the impact. The legs should rapidly be straightened and the whole body locked firmly upright, arms above the head. The gymnast who can achieve a rock-steady landing after a complex vault, without even a single staggering step, leaves a splendid impression on the judges.

It is the vaulting of great gymnasts that raises envy in the less talented spectator to its peak. Thousands may shriek with delight at the antics of Korbut on the floor, or hold their breath to see the incredible skills of Comaneci on the beam, but nothing draws such stunned envy as the explosive, super-human achievement of an outstanding vault. To most of us, it scarcely seems possible that the human frame can project itself so far with such complexity and such perfect grace. Those young and bold novices who long to try an advanced vault have constantly to be reminded that such an exercise is potentially very dangerous. Not only must such a gymnast be physically capable of such manoeuvres – and that means all-round development to a high degree – but he should understand, through his coach, at least some of the peculiar problems of body orientation in space, problems experienced to the full perhaps only by the trampolinist and the trapeze artist.

Be warned, eager and over-confident vaulters, that in no other gymnastic event can a misjudgment bring such savage retribution. In vaulting, you need to learn to walk for a long, long time before you start to run. And never, never try a vault without an experienced spotter on the other side of the horse. That said, it is time to look in more detail at some of the vaults that we see in top-class competition, those that are the goal of all vaulters to perfect.

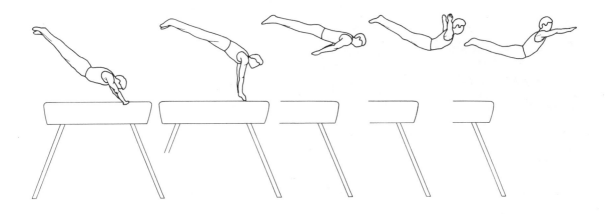

Handspring

There are very few vaults in international competition that do not involve the handstand, the basis of all the inverted vaults. The handspring, or long arm overthrow, is the simplest of these. Its mastery is the passport to an exciting world beyond, where that basic expertise can be refined and extended to incorporate even more dazzling tricks. It cannot be performed without a fast and confident approach, an explosive take-off and a long, high preflight. In advanced competition, men, using the long horse, vault off the far end, the neck. Before attempting that they will have perfected the handspring from the broad horse. Hand contact on the horse is made just before the body reaches the vertical in its preflight dive, and immediately, from this straight-arm handstand position, there is a powerful push-off. If there is not sufficient thrust at that moment, the postflight will be short and feeble instead of being long and elegant. The body in flight is absolutely straight, even slightly arched, with the arms fully extended above the head. The head moves slightly forward, on to the chest, to ensure sufficient body rotation for stable landing.

Yamashita

A Japanese male gymnast, Haruhiro Yamashita, is said to have first produced this vault in competition in 1962, though the world first marvelled at it during the Tokyo Olympics two years later. Basically it is a handspring vault with a 'pike' (a levering of the trunk and extended legs so that they make an angle of 90 degrees or less) in the postflight. Such has been the international progress of gymnastics over the past 15 years that this splendid vault, which was for a long time thought to be too difficult for women to attempt, is now a routine matter for most senior gymnasts of either sex, and no longer carries a particularly high tariff, i.e., the maximum points it is worth if correctly executed.

The primary phase differs from the plain handspring vault only in the angle at which contact is first made with the horse, which for the Yamashita is considerably flatter – probably about 45 degrees. This gives the performer fractionally more time for the pike, but nevertheless it has to be an extraordinarily rapid operation. The hips must begin moving the instant the hands touch the horse, which men's do at the neck, and

as the dynamic push-off is made, sending the vaulter up and on, the chest begins to close on the feet. There is probably less than a second in which to achieve the pike – and some close it tight, face almost touching knees – and open out again to full extension for landing. If the gymnast is late on the pike, he is almost certain to pitch forward on the mat. The power generated during this vital vault makes it necessary for the body to be angled back at least 10 degrees from the vertical on landing, to compensate for the impossibility of killing all its momentum without staggering. The Yamashita can be, and these days, often is, made more complex and more impressive by the introduction of twists or half twists. Without these, the Yamashita was the women's compulsory vault at the Montreal Olympics.

Tsukahara

Strictly for top-flight gymnasts, this is another forward-directional vault dependent on a handspring, but this time complicated by a half turn on the preflight, and a postflight requiring a one-and-a-half back somersault. The approach to the horse is in fact a cartwheel off the springboard, and one in which the performer continues to turn as his hands contact the horse. The push-off then occurs with the gymnast, upside down, facing the way he is going instead of the way he has come. The progress of the body continues, as usual, to be up and forward; but as the forward rotation produced by the cartwheel goes on, the knees are drawn up towards the chest for the one-and-a-half

Close-up view of a Tsukahara head-on. Korbut seems further advanced in her twist than usual at this stage, so the postflight was probably notably high

Sawao Kato (Japan), twice all-round Olympic champion

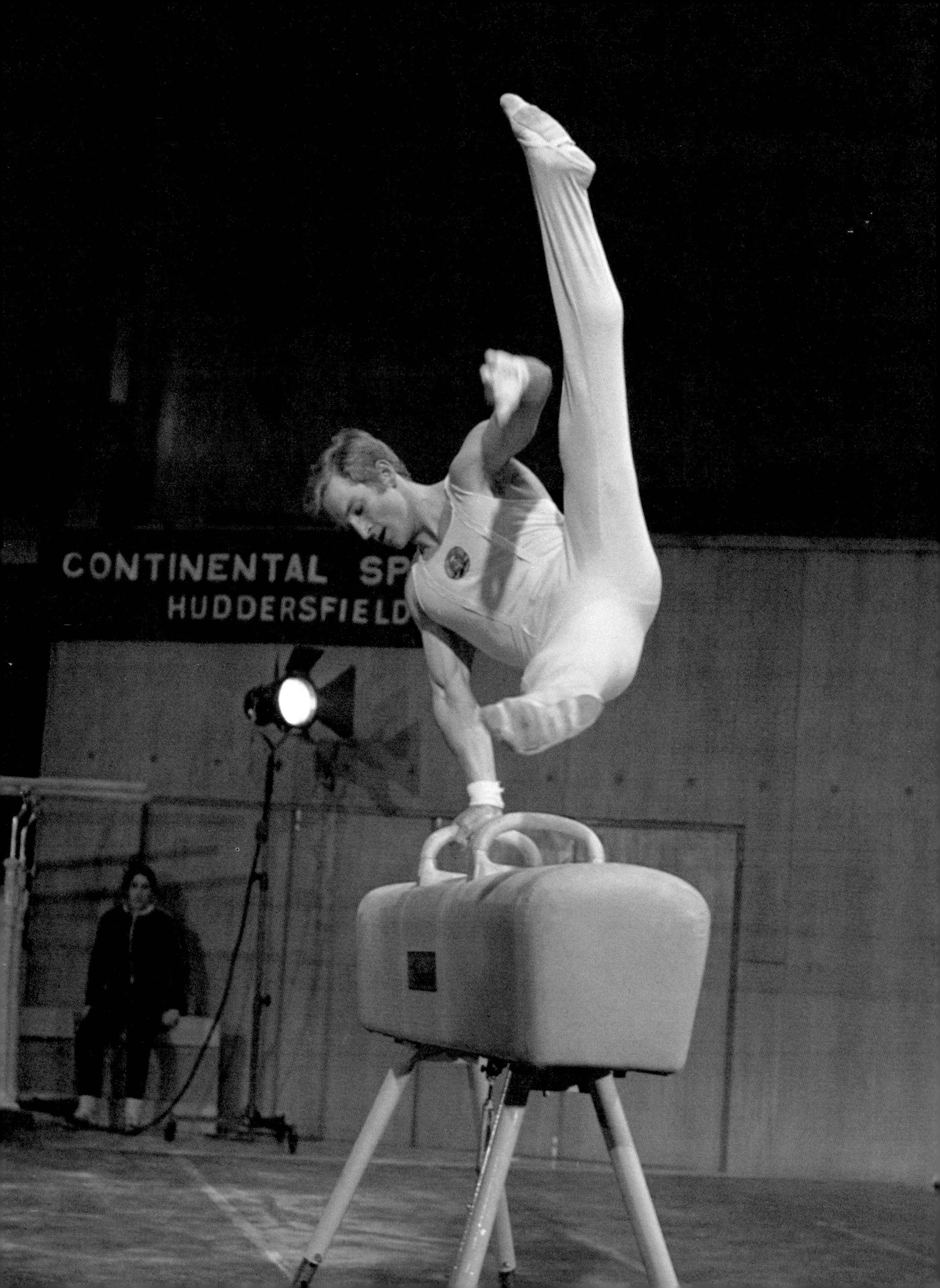
CONTINENTAL SP
HUDDERSFIELD

backward somersault that concludes with the Tsukahara master upright on his feet, facing the horse. It goes without saying that nobody tries this until his technical skill is highly-advanced and his determination and courage is of the highest order.

Stoop

A neat, reverse-directional vault that, at its simplest, is not particularly demanding and is regularly practised by gymnasts only just out of the novice class. Executed by experts, it is a work of art, and was the compulsory vault for men in the 1976 Olympics. The take-off needs to be quick and strong, and the preflight leads to contact with the horse (broadhorse for women, croup of the long horse for men) with the body extended and preferably slightly above the horizontal. Instantly the hips must move upward, as high as possible, and the feet come towards the hands with the legs straight. A forceful push-off sends the upper part of the body up to the horizontal and beyond as the legs, still straight, pass over the horse between the arms, in a more or less vertical position. The arms have in fact lost contact with the horse, and during the postflight are held out high to the side. With a long postflight, the expert achieves the characteristic full stretch of the whole body in descent.

Though that vault, without further elaboration, was the Olympic exercise, there are two major refinements often seen in international competition. The stoop with high preflight is an explosive vault that is highly rated, good to watch and difficult to control. The force necessary in take-off to produce the high preflight also produces a strong forward rotation of the body, which has to be halted and reversed – a technique requiring excellent coordination and timing. On contact with the horse, the body should be slightly arched, angled at about 45 degrees, and the hands well forward of the shoulders. The legs, which will have swung up as the hands braked the body's progress, are very quickly brought down and forward, and just as suddenly stopped when in the full stoop position. This, with the push-off and a raising of the head and shoulders, lifts the upper body and stops the forward rotation.

The piking action is unbelievably fast – indeed the whole vault seems to be over in a flash. Nevertheless, the expert manages to create time and space enough to achieve a fully-stretched postflight, thanks to the height a perfectly-timed push-off gives him.

On the long horse, experienced gymnasts can perform the giant stoop, the requirement for which is that instead of the preflight ending with the hands on the croup, they must go all the way to the neck of the horse. The full stretch of the slightly-arched body flying over the length of the horse is always an exciting sight, and in this vault in particular leads to a push-off requiring unusual strength. On contact, the body should be 30 degrees above the horizontal, and this 'racing dive' attitude is transformed in a fraction of a second to a close pike, high above the end of the horse. A startling manœuvre.

Hecht

The Hecht (usually seen as a giant Hecht, from the neck of the long horse) vault is among the most graceful yet devised, requiring the gymnast to operate throughout at full stretch, concluding the postflight in a 'swallow dive' position before going

The incredible all-rounder, Nikolai Andrianov (USSR)

into an upright landing. The fact that the body is fully extended both before and after push-off from the horse, makes the reversal of rotation particularly difficult to achieve. As in the giant stoop, the requirement is for a 30-degree approach; that degree of forward rotation has to be stopped and reversed without lowering the legs, by means of an exceptionally strong push-off with the hands. With the body well up and horizontal, the arms swing back and alongside the body, moving out to the full swallow-wing extension as the hips arch and the chest rises. Briefly, one has the impression of the gymnast gliding before the arms move forward again and the body completes its reverse rotation before landing.

By the time you read this book, other superb creations may have found their way into the schedule of the international gymnast, but they will almost certainly be based on those just discussed. All over the world, the greatest gymnasts are constantly trying to devise movements and combinations that have not yet been seen – as Yamashita did. Each time they do, all their rivals copy the new exercise and work on it until they can perform it as well as its originator does. If they do not, they may never catch up on the marks awarded for the difficulty and brilliance of the new vault. But behind all this scintillating sophistication, behind all these breathtaking performances that have made gymnastics one of the most popular spectator sports in the world, there lie years of routine practice at the basic vaults; hour after hour spent attempting to achieve perfection at vaults the public seldom see.

Squat

It is a matter of personal preference whether a coach starts you on the squat or the straddle. Neither are seen beyond elementary competition, both are still used as warm-up exercises by advanced gymnasts, and both give ample opportunity (as do all vaults) for refinement and the search for perfection. The squat vault requires the legs, with knees tightly bent, to pass between the arms as they push-off from the horse – which, at early stages will always be vaulted broadside on. The flights can be as high and long as you wish to make them, but the gymnast should aim at the body being extended and horizontal when the hands touch the horse. The hands will be in front of the shoulders, the arms straight, and at the instant of push-off the knees and hips begin to bend, bringing the thighs to a tucked position. As soon as the horse is cleared, the whole body stretches again, slightly arched, with the arms high overhead. Even though there is no element of postflight 'stunting' in these simple vaults, all descents should be at full stretch, and all landings cushioned by a slight bending at the knees and hips.

Straddle

When an expert performs the straddle vault, the preflight is high, bringing the body in at an angle of 45 degrees on contact. Push-off must be as slick and vigorous as ever, with the legs immediately spreading wide outside the arms. Head, chest and arms must rise right after push-off, helping to bring the body upright and stretched prior to landing. Both the straddle and the squat can be vaulted over a long horse, by those who can cope with it physically and psychologically, but the fundamentals must be mastered on a broad horse. Those who do move on to the long horse usually find it easier to start with a straddle, and to begin by vaulting from the neck (the far end). Though this requires a long, high preflight, that is generally easier to master than a vault from the croup, in which a particularly short preflight has to be followed by a long postflight. When learning croup vaulting, begin with the squat, not the straddle.

Flank vault

There are a number of ways of vaulting a horse that have no place in competition, but are very useful training exercises. The flank vault requires the gymnast to take a fairly short run with a vigorous take-off, contact the horse with both hands as usual, but immediately swing the legs to one side or the other and push off with one hand only – that on the side opposite to the one to which the legs swing. The swing, supported by that one arm, should be horizontal and well stretched, and the landing must be with the back to the horse. A variant on this is called a face vault, in which as the legs swing together over the horse, the body turns to face the horse, and the landing is made alongside the horse.

Thief vault

Not unlike the action of a track and field athlete in facing a hurdle or a high jump, this vault can be approached from the side (with the springboard suitably adjusted) or from face on. There is no preflight or postflight operation other than that required to clear the horse. As the gymnast hits the board, he performs a high scissors kick with the leg nearer the horse. The hand of the same side makes first contact with the horse,

Last word on vaulting from Nadia Comaneci, who performing in the Montreal optionals appears to be intent on going over the horse without touching it

and as the legs pass over the horse (straight and together), both hands support the body before pushing off to a stretched landing, back towards the horse.

A front approach poses greater problems. The take-off must be on one foot only. The leading leg is raised to pass over the horse, hurdle-fashion, before the hands make contact. Immediately from take-off, which must be very strong, the other leg swings up and out to catch up the leading leg before the horse is cleared. By the time of push-off, the body is well piked, and must extend again on the descent.

8 The Pommel Horse

Shall you admit, those who do not know much about gymnastics but do know what they like watching, that there is nothing more boring than the pommel horse? Sit through the average domestic competition and however brilliantly the men vault, however sensational they are on the rings, however smoothly they tackle the parallel bars, you can be sure half of them will come a cropper on the pommel horse. Whatever moments of embarrassment any of us can recall in our years of spectating, it is a fair bet that a third have come from seeing girls fall off the beam and two-thirds from seeing men grind to a halt over the pommels. No doubt about it, this is the exercise that sorts the men from the boys.

Known in many parts of the world as the side horse, the pommel horse has origins that go further back in history than any other piece of gymnastic equipment – back before Christ, to the training of mounted soldiers of the Roman army and on through the days of the knights in armour, when getting on a horse really was a job. It is exactly the same size as a vaulting horse, a maximum length of 5 feet 4 inches (1.62 m) and is kept at the height at which women vault, 3 feet 7 inches (1.09 m). The only difference is that across the centre of the horse, about 1 foot 5 inches (43 cm) apart, is a pair of rigid handles. They are bolted through the body of the horse, rise to 4¾ inches (12 cm) above its upper surface, and comfortably accommodate the gymnast's hands – both hands in one handle if he wishes. These pommels take the entire swinging weight of the gymnast, who should not touch any part of the horse except with his hands.

The vaulting horse is divided theoretically into three sections – croup, saddle and neck. In this event, the presence of the pommels makes the division a practical one, and the neck is always the end that is on the gymnast's left as he approaches the horse. All three parts of the horse must be used during a routine. Illustrations in a German manual of gymnastics of 1845 show the horse with an unmistakable neck, sloping considerably upwards. That goes at least some way towards explaining why double-leg circles, now the staple diet of the pommel performer, were not introduced until 1868.

The style of execution of pommel horse exercises differs from any other of the gymnastic disciplines. In all others there is, to some degree, a sense of freedom; the performer is encouraged, and sometimes required, to vary the tempo of his work. On the pommels the gymnast must do nothing of the kind: he must never stop, he must never pause, and he must operate from beginning to end at a constant speed. Increasing and decreasing the speed of the leg circles that occupy most of the gymnast's time wins him nothing but a thumbs down. In a sense, the performer needs to be boring to do the job perfectly: this is not an occasion for a display of extrovert personality, or spontaneity, or even of flair. The master of the pommel horse is a man of discipline, concentration and perfect order.

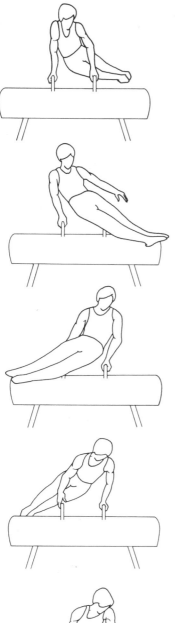

Physically, he is most likely to succeed if he is taller than average, with long arms and exceptional arm and shoulder strength. It is not possible for a man without sufficient strength to perform well on the pommels; but strength alone will not win the day. The legs in their everlasting travels must always be swung, never lifted; nor is the swinging confined to the legs. Watch the greatest performers and see that their movements originate not at the hips, but at the shoulders. The whole body swings, but the legs swing

The origins of the pommel horse go back 2000 years, to wooden horses for training Roman soldiers; after that, to mounting exercises for knights in armour

7 LEFT: Pommel horse: double leg circle

73

The three sections of the horse are called neck, saddle and croup. A hundred years ago the neck used to slope up and a horse's head was painted on it

more. And above all the swinging and the strength comes the key to the whole performance, the word that would be obvious if you froze the movement at any point in a top-class routine: balance. The man who concedes the slightest loss of balance is unlikely to find that his strength alone can prevent him colliding with the body of the horse, or even collapsing over it.

So perhaps it is not such a dull exercise after all? British coach Nik Stuart says it is 'probably the most fascinating piece of apparatus in the Olympic range'. Once the gymnast has mastered the rhythm of the double-leg circles, he says, interest is rarely lost, and there are many gymnasts who practise on the pommels to the exclusion of everything else, for the sheer love of it. It is an undeniable problem that the apparently inevitable lack of immediate success on the pommels does dishearten the beginner – who, if he is young, may not at that stage be strong enough to cope with the apparatus. Even given the strength, the perseverance and patience needed to master the technique is immense. You cannot help being slightly discouraged, perhaps, to learn from a Japanese master of the art that until you have spent several years developing the skill of circling, you cannot say that you have even the makings of a champion!

Perfection is a splendid goal, but in this event above all, it is important not to seek it too soon. The beginner should set up a target he knows he can hit; when he hits it, he can erect the next one further away. Everybody needs the excitement of success to inspire the next, and greater, effort. For instance, a youngster who wants to get to grips with the pommel horse should prepare himself by working on the more familiar parallel bars. By walking the body backwards and forwards in straight arm support on the two bars, by travelling down one bar sideways, by passing the weight of the body from one hand to the other in support on the bars, he can begin to build up his physical tolerance. Then he can become familiar with the new apparatus by using it for simple squat vaults through the pommels, flank vaults, thief vaults and that sort of thing.

Nearly all the basic pommel swings are performed from one of three support positions – which, as on the parallel bars, means that the hands grasp a pommel each, the arms are straight and the shoulders are above the hands: in front support, the gymnast is facing the horse; in back support, he has his back to it; in straddle support, he has one leg on each side of the horse between the pommels. When he feels ready to start his pommel operations, the gymnast could begin in front support by simply swinging to the left and right, concentrating on letting the whole body swing from the shoulders. As the leading leg gets higher and higher to each side, the gymnast should take that hand off the pommel at the top of the swing, balancing on the other one. The exercise can be carried out not just from the pommels, but all the way along the horse, neck to croup, and in back support as well as front.

Next, he can try a 'cut in'. This is a very familiar move in which, while swinging in front support to the left, the performer takes his left hand off the pommel and swings his right leg through the gap and over the horse, regrasping the pommel so that he ends in straddle support. When this too has been practised on both sides, the next move should be to start in straddle support and cut the rear leg in, to end in rear support. From front support again, the gymnast can then put together a few flowing movements: left leg in, left leg out; right leg in, right leg out ('out' is the opposite of 'in', with the leg passing back under a raised hand to the rear of the horse again). When he can do that from back support as well as front, the beginner can give a name to these basic exercises and move from the first time to the magic word 'circles'.

Single leg half-circle

The gymnast now needs to start with an official take-off, standing in front of the horse with his hands on the pommels. The

World and Olympic champion Zoltan Magyar (Hungary), greatest pommel artist of the decade, on a double-leg circle with his own special variety of travel

take-off jump sends his legs swinging to the left. As they swing more strongly to the right, he removes his right hand with a firm push-off, raises it and swings the right leg over the pommel into straddle, immediately regrasping the pommel. In straddle, the right leg swings forward and back, the right hand pushes off again and the right leg swings back over the horse. He regrasps in front support and has completed a single leg half-circle. Next time, when he returns to his starting position, he will let the swing go on to the left side and do a half circle from there; and after that, he will do it from back support. You may notice we have used the word swing six times in those few lines: that

75

Nikolai Andrianov 'cutting out' in a beautifully-defined forward scissors. See how the sharpness of his trouser creases contributes to the movement

is what it is all about – a ceaseless, flowing swing all around the horse, with the leg only crossing the horse when the swing has taken it to its highest point.

Single leg circles

A basic single leg circle from front support requires the gymnast to swing high to the right, push off with the right hand, turn the hips slightly forward to move the right leg over the horse and regrasp the pommel. As the swing in straddle support reaches high to the left, and remember the rear leg is swinging too, the left hand pushes off, the swing reaches its peak and, with another slight adjustment of the hips, the right leg comes over the horse again. The left hand immediately regrasps the pommel and the body swings to the right in front support.

In what is called an undercut single leg circle, still from front support, the body circles in the same direction but it is the other leg that comes over the horse. This time, as the legs swing high to the right and the right hand pushes off, the hips turn to the right, the left leg straddles the horse and continues to swing to the left. The right hand has regrasped the pommel as soon as possible, the right arm stiffens to take the weight, the left arm pushes off and the left

The further over the supporting hand the shoulder can be, the better the balance. Here the right leg is admirably high as the left passes over the horse

leg swings back over the horse. The undercut circle requires greater hip flexibility, and it is almost needless to say that, like all other circles, it must be practised with both legs and from all parts of the horse – not just from the saddle. The technique remains the same.

Circling gets a little more tricky in back support. Though we talk about the movement as if it were starting from a static back support position, the necessary swing could not be engendered from there, so one must imagine that immediately before that moment, the legs have swung down and have momentum. They are swinging high to the gymnast's left, the horse is now behind him, the weight shifts on to the right arm, the left hand pushes off, the hips turn

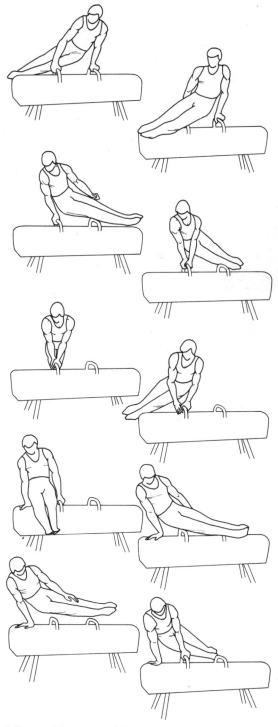

8 Pommel horse: double leg circle with side travel

77

Pommel exercises must be evenly rhythmic and ceaseless. Breaking the diet of scissors and double-leg circles, a flashy single-leg circle in back support

and the left leg swings over the top. The left hand regrasps the pommel, the legs continue swinging in straddle support, the left arm takes the weight and the right arm pushes off. It is very important now that the leg that is still in front of the horse, the right, swings as high as possible, because the left leg is coming over the horse underneath it – or to be more accurate, at a moment when the left hip is under the right hip. The right hand regrasps and the gymnast is in his back support position again.

To perform an undercut single leg circle in back support is to be knocking on the door of double leg circles, so it deserves the greatest attention and practice. Very considerable speed is needed to the first section of the swing, for at the top of the swing to

9 Pommel horse: forward scissors

the gymnast's left, when the left hand has pushed off, the right leg has to move backward over the horse, underneath the left leg. The left hand returns to the pommel, the straddle swing is on, the right hand releases and the right leg comes over the horse to the front again. Though that does not sound too bad, the gymnast has to be determined to get a good swing on both legs, and not to adjust the hips until the swing has reached its peak – otherwise the leg that is circling will hit the horse.

Scissors

You cannot perform a competitive routine without including both forward and reverse (or front and back) scissors, and though it takes an expert to execute a really high scissors to perfection, the beginner should start to work on the move as soon as he is happy about all his basic support swings. It is an attractive, rhythmic movement involving very high swinging from the hips. Starting from a front support, the gymnast performs a single leg half-circle with his right leg, swinging it particularly high before bringing it over the horse. The right leg continues its swing to the left in the straddle support position, while the left leg, as usual, also swings to the left on the other side of the horse. After it has passed the horizontal, the left hand pushes off and is swung swiftly up, helping the left leg to increase the power of its swing, which must be to an astonishing height. Get it as high as it will go, the coaches tell you, and then another foot or two. At that stage, the right leg is also high enough to clear the horse, and the hips are brought forward over the horse so that the right leg can cut out to the gymnast's side of the horse just before the left leg comes

down from its peak and cuts in to the straddle. The support swing continues, with both legs swinging to the right – the left leg, straddled, to the horizontal and the right leg swung high to the skies. Every aspect of the move must be polished if it is to succeed, but perhaps no part of it is more important than to have the hips over the horse, not behind it, at the time the 'scissor' is being executed.

In the reverse scissors it is the forward leg that rises high before cutting out (that is, passing back over the horse) and the back leg that, at the same time, moves low forward under the raised hand and cuts in. So the pattern is that, in straddle support, the left leg is forward and swinging left. When it is about to make contact with the left arm, the left hand leaves the pommel and is raised. The left leg goes on rising high, the hips are moved in over the horse and the right leg, which has swung up behind the horse until it is horizontal and clear of it, passes to the front. As soon as it has cleared the pommel, the left hand grasps it again and the swing to the right in straddle support continues, with the right leg now on the far side of the horse.

Double leg circles

The pommel horse routine is so dominated by double leg circles, it is not surprising that some gymnasts are deluded into thinking there is no other move they need bother to practise. Single leg techniques must be kept polished, though one can hardly deny that the man who can perfect a sequence of varied double leg circles without tiring is the man likely to come off with a high score. Certainly nobody who fails to master this exacting technique will become a

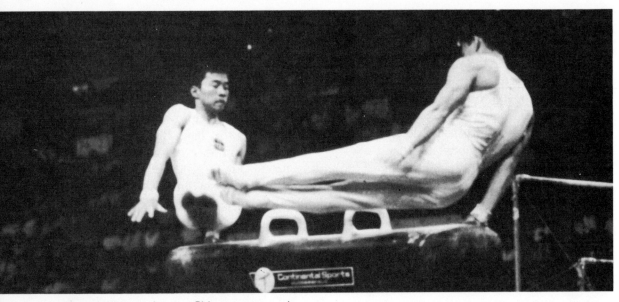

For exhibition only: two Chinese gymnasts in London in a rare double act, managing to execute double-leg circles together without kicking each other off

world-class gymnast, and the novice needs to spend many hours, though only a few minutes at a time, practising double leg movements that will lead him towards the circle – or rather, towards a series of circles executed at constant rhythm, for that is where so many good gymnasts fail. As Nik Stuart indicated, once you have got it, you are through the barrier; gymnastic life suddenly looks brighter.

It is clear what the gymnast is aiming at: a series of circles in which the legs remain together and fully extended, moving round and round over the horse in an approximately horizontal plane, cutting in and out of the pommel grips as they go. It is a very punishing exercise throughout the long period it usually takes to master it. Assume the gymnast is circling clockwise. His first move, having acquired the necessary swing, is to cut both legs left in – that is, to bring

them forward over the left side of the horse (the neck), under his raised left arm. Unless he guards against it, he will find a tendency to bend at the hips and let his head drop down on his chest. What is needed is not a bend, but a twist: just before the legs cut in, the performer's shoulders are square on, both hands gripping the pommels; but the legs are approaching the horse, on his left. By the time the feet have swung out to the front of the horse, when many gymnasts go into a pike the body should be almost straight from toes to shoulders, at an angle of about 30 degrees to the horizontal. At this point the body has to be well back to maintain balance.

As the swing continues to the right, the legs must twist up to clear the horse – but again, the hips should be neither bent nor lifted. So it cuts right out, passing under the raised right arm to the rear of the horse and untwisting as it goes. When the line of the body is at right angles to the line of the horse, the body is absolutely straight, the head back, the shoulders forward. And so it swings on to the left again.

At all times the arms and legs must be straight and the whole body stretched as much as possible. To prevent the legs from overbalancing the body, as they want to, the gymnast must lean well over the support hand. He will have worked on double leg circles on the pommels for a long time before he ventures on to either end of the horse for the same movement, but it must be done: then, the counter-balancing necessary to clear the legs over the pommels becomes even greater.

Travel

When the gymnast has mastered double leg circles on all parts of the horse, he will want to try to do them on the move. The simplest technique for this is known as side travel, involving a double leg circle that starts on the pommels and finishes at one end of the horse, still in front support. There are two movements in particular, based on side travel, that are popular with advanced gymnasts: the stockli, in which while he travels the performer reverses the direction in which he is facing before returning to his original position; and the tromlet, in which he begins as usual in front support, travels to the end and back again, and finishes on the same side of the horse but in back support.

When aiming to travel right, the gymnast cuts his legs in under his right arm, then out under his left. At that moment his weight is well over the right pommel, which as soon as his legs are through he grasps with the left hand as well as the right. As the legs are cut in for the second time, the body, supported by the left arm on the right pommel,

is moving over the right end of the horse. The right hand comes down on the near side of the horse, fingers pointing to the right end, and the left arm is lifted to allow the legs to cut out over the pommels.

The stockli begins with a basic double leg circle. As it is completed and the second one begins, the performer is looking down at the left end of the horse, to which he is going to travel. His legs cut in on the right, and as they swing across the far side of the horse, the gymnast is rolling his hips to the left, pressing them tightly against the supporting arm. As the legs swing over the left end of the horse, the upper body and right arm follow them, pivoting on the left arm, so that by the time the right hand comes down on the horse the gymnast is in back support. When the legs have cut in again over the pommels and the gymnast has regrasped what was the left (neck side) pommel with his left hand, he is in fact in front support on the far side of the horse, but looking towards the saddle, to his left, in preparation for the next circle. Again the body leans heavily on the pivot arm, the hips pressing against it. The whole body swings round the end of the horse, the legs continue over the saddle, the gymnast, whose left hand is still grasping the left pommel, takes the right pommel with his right hand and he is back on a standard double leg circle again. The major difficulty in both the stockli and the tromlet is to maintain balance while turning on one arm. The more firmly the body and the arm press together the better that will be accomplished.

The tromlet begins with a standard double leg circle in side travel. When the performer has reached the right end of the horse, in front support, he pushes off with the outside arm and leans over the pivot

Veteran of two Olympics, Stan Wild was for years Britain's national champion and best-known competitor, but he was never maestro of the pommel horse

Mounts and dismounts

There are no hard and fast rules for beginning or ending an exercise on the pommel horse. As with the parallel bars and the balance beam, the start and finish need to be clean and slick, and the advanced gymnast will usually devise a spectacular dismount on the reasonable supposition that the best time to impress the judges is immediately before they award the marks. The beginner should concentrate on moving smoothly from his last stunt into a crisp dismount that leaves him standing upright, without stumbling, beside the horse. A simple and popular opening for the novice is some form of kehre mount, which he begins by standing with his left hand on the neck of the horse and his right on the pommel. He can then take off to an immediate single or double leg circle, going either over the neck or the saddle, to leave himself in a front support position on the saddle or, with the single leg kehre, in straddle support.

arm on the pommel. As his legs continue the circle, his body pivots with them. As soon as they have passed over the pommels, which the left hand has continued to grip, he grasps the other pommel with his right hand. The gymnast is then balanced over the saddle in back support. Once again, the positioning of the outside hand is vitally important: it must be placed on the near side of the horse.

9 Parallel Bars

Few spectators would pick the parallel bars as the scene of their favourite gymnastic event, but to many male gymnasts this is the most interesting piece of equipment of them all. In modern times work on the parallel bars has moved away from the demonstration of strength it once was, to a fluent, flowing exhibition of swinging and suppleness, of balance and boldness. Because the bars can so easily be adjusted within a great range of heights, they make an admirable introduction to gymnastic activity – even to the very young; and they have the advantage that, at any stage of progress or expertise, exercises can be practised with the bars set low.

The German father-figure of gymnastics, Jahn, certainly did not anticipate that the parallel bars, which he invented in 1812, would turn out to be the kingdom of the smaller, supple man whose strength/weight ratio might be on the low side. He created them primarily to serve a great master, the pommel horse, at that time the most popular item in his Berlin gymnasium. Jahn's overriding interest was in strength, and his bars were first used for preparatory exercises to build up shoulder muscle that would enable support swinging on the pommels to be more expertly undertaken.

His early bars were seized by soldiers for firewood during the Napoleonic war, and their replacements were stolen. After the war, neither the parallel bars nor the horizontal bar, which he also invented, figured prominently in competition. But Jahn's determination prevailed: his groups of travelling gymnasts popularized the parallel bars all over Germany. By 1850 they had become adjustable in height, women were using them, and so sophisticated had become the exercises that a swing to handstand was already being perfected. Within ten years most of the moves that we see on the bars today were commonplace.

Perhaps because of the great popularity of the bars, they were singled out for particular attack in the 1860s, after Jahn's death. The devotees of the opposing gymnastic system, Ling's Swedish school of free movement, were unhampered by equipment. Among the allegations flung at the parallel bars was that they caused such anatomical deformations as hunchbacks. Whether under the influence of such attacks or not, the emphasis in bars work did slowly change. The twentieth century brought the elimination of most of the slow moves that depended solely on strength, and their replacement by exercises in which swing was all-important. There followed, almost inevitably, a basic technical change in the bars themselves: they became thinner and flexible, making it almost impossible to achieve body movement by strength alone.

Today the parallel bars are approximately 11 feet 6 inches (3.4 m) long, and their supports are 7 feet 6 inches (2.3 m) apart. The bars are almost egg-shaped in cross-section, two inches deep and one-and-a-half inches wide at the most, with a flatly-rounded upper surface and a slightly more conical shape at the bottom. In competition, they are set 5 feet 7 inches (1.7 m)

Now primarily an instrument of swinging, Kurt Jahn created the parallel bars to develop strength. Here Bill Norgrove (GB) sits in the popular half-lever

less pure strength than the rings, less nerve than the high bar and less sudden decision than the vault, but represent a positive stabilization of all these virtues combined. Certainly it is the all-rounder's apparatus: in the six Olympic Games between 1956 and 1976, the champion gymnast was twice the man who won the floor exercises, twice the man who won the vault, once the winner of the rings. Never in that time were the champions of the horizontal bar, or the pommel horse the all-round champions, but four times the winner on the parallel bars proved to be the supreme competitor of the Olympics.

On no other piece of equipment can the gymnast produce such a rich diversity of movement, and even the novice finds it, says Kunzle, 'relatively easy to propel himself into, and hold himself in, that divine position which is the envy of man and the prerogative of angels, fully extended, upside down, enthroned above the world'. Which is, you must agree, an exciting way of describing a handstand on the parallel bars.

A swing into handstand is probably the most important move to master. Certainly you will see no routine, either compulsory or voluntary, without one. A competitor is only allowed to 'freeze' three times in any routine, and the handstand is likely to provide one or two of those moments. Many performances either start or finish with one, and those who can, move on to twisting and turning handstands. Before we examine those techniques in more detail, it is time to look at basics.

Those of us who enjoy watching gymnastics but do not practise them tend not to concentrate much on the parallel bars. It perhaps seems a bit of a muddle, and the

above floor level, making it impossible for the gymnast to hang below them with arms and body extended. They are the most responsive of all gymnastic apparatus, with a considerably complex physical character. The behaviour of bars can vary almost from set to set, and certainly from one manufacturer to another, making the warm-up period before competition particularly vital.

Men's competitions often begin with the parallel bars exercises. In his definitive work, *Parallel Bars*, G. C. Kunzle suggests this is perhaps because the bars require less delicacy of balance than the pommel horse,

One of the greatest performers on the bars, world and Olympic silver medallist Nikolai Andrianov of the USSR shows the real meaning of 'full extension'

bars get in the way, and anyway it is all over in a few seconds; events like the vault and the rings and the high bar and the floor exercises are out in the open, clear and exciting to see, and occupy most of our attention. All that is true enough, but as a spectator you will enrich your enjoyment infinitely if you do watch the bars carefully, analyse the movements and see what has been accomplished.

There are really only three ways of holding yourself on the parallel bars, and they are known in the business as support, hang, and upper arm hang or upper arm support.

You cannot perform without being fluent in all positions, but of the three, support is the controlling and most common one. That name is given to any movement and position in which the shoulders are above the hands, and is most commonly seen when the gymnast's body is hanging between the bars, supported by straight arms.

Hang covers all times when the gymnast's body is below the bars. You will often see it with the body fully extended and more or less horizontal, the hands grasping the bars above the shoulders. In upper arm hang, or upper arm support, the shoulders and hands are level on the bars, which is why some call it one thing and some the other. It is much the most awkward position

It looks too late for Alexander Detiatin to complete his twist and regrasp the bars, but the body is still rising and the Russian's poise is undisturbed

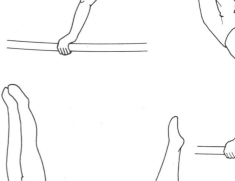

10 Parallel bars: Stutze

in which the beginner finds himself, an unnatural position and unique to this
apparatus, but it must be done: the upper
arms rest on top of the bars, taking the
weight of the body. The hands lie on the
bars, but cannot contribute greatly at that
stage. Upper arm support swinging is something that has to be learned, and sometimes
painfully. Our upper arms are not accus-
tomed to such rough treatment, and until
the skin there toughens up they may well
protest at the violent rubbing they are
given.

Support swing

Swinging is the heart of 90 per cent of
parallel bars work (a competitive routine
has to show only one move of strength), and
simple swings in all three basic positions
must be perfected before the gymnast can
move on to impressive stunts. The support
swing is the most natural to start with, but
it is not as easy to swing smoothly as it looks.
Beginners tend to buckle at the arms, which
must always be locked straight, and to let
their shoulders move back and forwards too
much with the swings. This alters the centre
of gravity too sharply and produces an unstable swing.

On the back swing, the shoulders should
be slightly in front of the hands, on the front
swing slightly behind them. The head must
always be held up, the chest full, and the
aim should be to keep the body stretched
and the toes pointed. There will in fact be
an arching at the top of the back swing and
a piking on the front swing, but it must be
kept under control.

Upper arm support swing

In his book *Olympic Gymnastics*, Akitomo
Kaneko gives some excellent tips for 'breaking in' the upper arms before the beginner
attempts to swing. He advises the young
gymnast to get into upper arm support, then
raise and lower the body by moving the
shoulders up and down. It might hurt at
first, he says, but eventually you will be able
to tolerate it! When he is used to that, the
novice can try jumping backwards and forwards on the bars, from the same position.
All coaches are agreed that the initial swinging should be gentle – little and often is the
key.

In a pure upper arm support swing, the
upper arm must remain in contact with the
bars, so the chest does not rise above the
horizontal on forward or backward swings.
At the top of the back swing the shoulders
are as high as possible and the body
extended. Just before it reaches the vertical
on the downward and forward movement,
a slight flexing of the hips helps to send it
strongly up, in the same way that it does on
the playground swing. Similarly, a forceful
arching of the body on the back swing gives
it impetus for the rest of the journey, which
is helped by the upper arms pressing down
on the bar.

As a practice routine, the novice may find
it useful to combine support and upper arm
support swings, by starting in support,
swinging back to a good high extension,
then down into the upper arm support, continuing the forward swing; and vice versa,
starting with a front support swing and ending with a back upper arm swing.

11 Parallel bars: support swing

A swing in upper-arm support. Novice gymnasts must break in gently the tender area of the body that bears the unaccustomed friction of this exercise

Hang swings

Kaneko recommends practising hang swinging from a horizontal bar, set low. This enables the gymnast to get the feel of circling in both directions before attempting to do it in the less natural confinement of the parallel bars. In almost all hang swings, because of the lack of space between the gymnast and the floor, the legs spend much of the time bent at the hips. As the performer advances to more sophisticated moves, he will often find himself using a bent inverted hang swing – which in itself is not as bad as it sounds. The gymnast hangs from the bar, using an inside grip with straight arms. The legs, which are also

straight, are piked tightly over his body, in a horizontal position. By vigorously opening the legs from the pike to about 90 degrees, and at the same time pulling on the bars with the arms still extended, the gymnast can swing his body back and up. He immediately pikes it again for the down swing, opening again and pulling as the body passes the vertical on its way forward.

With those simple swings confidently and smoothly mastered, the gymnast can move on to stage two of his parallel bar education: forward and backward uprises, forward and backward rolls, the shoulder stand and the handstand.

Uprises

Uprises are extensions of upper arm support swings. The back uprise begins with the body at the peak of a forward swing and ends with it at the peak of a back support swing, with arms straight. The momentum needed to provide the full uprise is produced by ensuring that, in the forward swing position, the hips are fully stretched and that, as the body swings down, the hips are slightly bent and lead the body. As the body flies back into its full extension, well above the bars, the hands must have a good grip of the bars and the shoulders should be slightly in front of the hands.

That in itself is a satisfactory exercise for anyone in the early stages of parallel bar work, but in practice the back uprise is used as a means of reaching a new position, such as a shoulder stand or handstand. In such cases, the momentum must be great in the downswing, the body must be strongly arched as it travels back and up, and the hands must pull strongly on the bars to keep the shoulders close. It is very difficult to bring the legs up to the vertical if the body is allowed to extend fully.

After that, the front uprise needs little explanation. It begins at the peak of an

On the way down in a Stutze – the impressive move in which the gymnast rises with a forward swing, lets go of the bars and half-twists to a handstand

When strength was everything, bars were built to take an elephant without flinching. Today they are flexible, giving impetus to swinging and mobility

upper arm support back swing, and needs precise technique and considerable strength to execute. As the upper arm swing reaches its highest level to the front, the arms are vigorously straightened, the chest and body fully extended. The Japanese technique, which is most impressive, is to climax the

front uprise with the shoulders stretched straight up above the hands, the chest horizontal and the legs bent at the hips and extended fully in the vertical position.

A very useful variant on the front uprise, and one which requires and develops great shoulder and arm strength, is to incorporate

Mitsuo Tsukahara's name will live through his vault; he ensured his place in history by winning the overall and the bars bronze medals at Montreal

a dip swing. This time the movement cannot begin on an upper arm swing. At the top of the back swing the arms must be in the full support position, and as the downward and forward swing begins, the gymnast must bend his arms at the elbow. The bend must be completed before the body reaches the vertical, and the arms must be fully straightened again by the time the body reaches the limit of its forward swing. It is important that before the dip swing front uprise is attempted, the shoulder and arm muscles should be well developed. Incorrectly executed, it can lead to shoulder muscle strain.

Rolls

The forward roll starts with a support swing and ends with an upper arm support swing. It is an uncomplicated movement, the timing of which is soon acquired, but if the gymnast is not to fall through the bars he must never forget to keep his elbows out!

From the back swing in support, the body is piked and rotated forward. When the shoulders come into contact with the bars, the hands release their grip (elbows out), the body is straightened and the hands regrasp at the earliest opportunity, in the upper arm support position. The head should be held up at the start of the movement, tucked into the chest as soon as the roll commences, and lifted as soon as it is over.

Upper arm support begins and ends the backward roll. It opens with a full forward swing in upper arm support, with a greater stretch at the start, a slight arching as the body reaches vertical and a jerking forward and upward of the legs as soon as the vertical is passed. As the body rises under this added momentum, it is stretched out of its slightly piked state, the head is thrown back and the hands leave the bars to extend fully sideways. If they are not extended, the body will fall between the bars as it comes up to the vertical over the top. As the backward roll is completed, the hands regrasp the bars in the upper arm support again, continuing the forward swing.

The backward roll can be used to take the

gymnast into a shoulder stand, a full support swing (master the shoulder stand first) or a handstand. The last, known as the Strelli, is not for novices.

Shoulder stand

When the young gymnast can perform the rolls confidently, he will not find it difficult to master the shoulder stand. It should first be practised statically, perhaps from a straddle sit position on the bars, with the hands placed in front of the legs. The performer can lower his shoulders to the bars, about a foot in front of the hands, lift the hips above the head and follow with the legs. The head needs to be kept back and the back slightly arched to maintain balance.

When this position is reached from any kind of swinging move, considerable technical mastery is needed to counteract the fact that more weight is immediately placed on the shoulders. It should go without saying that no move of this kind should be tried without the assistance of a coach or experienced spotter.

Handstand

Everybody knows what a handstand is. On the floor, it usually presents the first and most eagerly accepted challenge in a child's physical education. Of course, the handstand must be infallibly mastered on the floor before any gymnast tries it on the bars, but with that understood, it does not present too many problems. The beginner should try it on support bars on the ground, and then on the end of the parallel bars, with the hands and feet on the bars as if they were on the floor. It is obviously important that anyone doing a handstand on the bars should know what they are going to do if they lose their balance. It is not a pleasant thing for the inexperienced gymnast to do, and needless accidents do happen from sheer fright. Coaches usually train their charges to drop into a shoulder stand, and on to a forward roll, which is a very neat way out of trouble.

Experienced gymnasts explore variations of that straightforward handstand on two bars — known as a parallel handstand, because the body, if it swung down, would be parallel with the bars. A parallel handstand can also be performed on a single bar, one hand close in front of the other; or a perpendicular handstand can be performed on one bar, the hands shoulders' width apart and side by side, so that the shoulders are parallel to one bar but the body, if it dropped, would be across the bars. A Swiss handstand is frequently used by advanced performers as their strength move: the arms and trunk must remain rock steady as the legs, bent from the hips and straddled, are raised to the vertical and back again. Those with exceptional strength and perfect balance can demonstrate a one-armed handstand, and the greatest of them all do it with the legs together — straddling them makes balancing slightly easier. It is probably the most impressive static position you will see on the bars — gloriously impossible, you might think. So is the Moore, though some manage it without trouble: a backward swing from support into handstand; then a quarter turn to one side, both hands on the same bar; and a quarter turn again to both bars, facing the opposite direction to that in which you started. Gymnasts who no longer find that a problem perform the hair-raising feat of removing both hands

Most exciting of bars moves, the flying backward roll is executed by former British champion Tommy Wilson. He somersaults from handstand to handstand

from the bars at the same time while making the first turn.

Ignoring such advanced refinements, the embryo artist on the parallel bars is now theoretically equipped to begin rhythmically putting together a routine. He can swing in the three basic positions, can

uprise and roll backwards and forwards, and can achieve a steady handstand and shoulder stand. It is in the smooth and fluent stitching together of all the elements of his performance, without pausing, that the gymnast achieves success on the bars. Given that, and without removing his routine from one of absolute simplicity, there is still one important problem for him to solve: how to get down.

Dismounts

Bringing a performance to an impressive conclusion, and one that leaves the gymnast securely and elegantly on his feet by the apparatus, is likely to be his most important single achievement. At the elementary level, he can perform a front or back dismount from a simple support swing. At the very peak of a backward support swing, he transfers his weight to the arm on his dismount side, brings the other hand over and grasps the bar just in front of the arm that is supporting him. As the body moves from the vertical plane between the bars and passes to one side, the performer shifts his weight back to the other arm, swings the free arm up and sideways, and lets the stretched body swing to the ground, head and chest held high. He tries to land lightly, with his shoulders at right angles to the bars.

That is the front dismount. A back dismount is made from a front support swing in similar manner, except that the shifting of weight to the arm on the dismount side occurs not at the peak of the swing, but as soon as the body is past the vertical. The hand from the far side comes across behind the body to grasp the dismount bar, the free arm stretches sideways and the legs and body swing together over the bar and to the ground.

In a flank dismount, the body bends at the hips halfway through a front support swing. The gymnast pushes off with the arm opposite the dismount side, the shoulders turn and the body pivots on the dismount arm, which must be kept straight. As the body passes over the bar, it straightens again and the performer lands with his back to the bars.

Slightly more adventurous, the front dismount through a handstand: the gymnast rises to a handstand from a strong back support swing. Just before he reaches the handstand, he leans slightly to the dismount side, pushes with the opposite arm and turns his head towards the dismount. As the body turns in the air, the opposite hand comes over to grasp the dismount bar and become the pivot on which the body swings over the bar and forward for a landing beside it.

If the gymnast contrives to conclude his performance at the end of the bars, he can use a straddle dismount. For this he needs a long, high back support swing. Just before its peak he bends his hips and leans forward, so that his shoulders are in front of his hands. He then needs a strong push off, opening his legs wide to the straddle. Once clear of the bars, the landing should be with a well-stretched, slightly arched body.

It would be absurd to pretend that in the past few pages we have done more than suggest a few of the almost infinite variety of movements and positions of which the parallel bar gymnast is capable. One strength position that you will almost certainly see in any experienced performer's routine, for example, is some form of L-support. In this, with the arms in straight support, the legs are slowly raised to exactly 90 degrees – either close together, or in straddle. And if you watch carefully the performance of an expert, you are fairly sure to see, somewhere amid the twists and turns and the underbar and overbar somersaults, these four sophisticated swinging stunts: the kip, the cast, the Stutze and the Strelli.

Kip

A popular means of raising the body from any kind of hang position to any kind of support position. At the peak of a vigorous forward hang swing, the legs are quickly bent at the hips into an inverted pike. Still hanging, the gymnast swings backwards, his legs over his head, and then pulls strongly on the bars, thrusting the hips up. Ideally, the legs stretch up vertically and the arms are in full support.

Cast

This is not far removed from the reverse of a kip. It begins in support and moves through inverted pike hang to upper arm support, and sometimes back to support again. From a forward swing in support, the gymnast drops into the inverted pike hang, tightly closed. He immediately swings the legs up and forward and pulls strongly on the bars, lifting the whole body until the shoulders are just above the bars. He can then move his arms sideways, ready to regrasp the bar in upper arm support, and stretches his legs forward. From the resulting backward swing, the straight arm support can be reached again.

Stutze

An impressive stunt originating from a vigorous forward support swing, led with the feet. When the legs have passed the horizontal, the performer lets go with one hand, pivoting on the other arm into a quarter turn. The feet and legs are still swinging up, enabling him to release his grip on the bar altogether, completing the half turn, regrasping the bars and continuing, usually, into a handstand. No top-class competition is likely to be without a Stutze, and the exceptionally talented gymnast may turn it into a Diomidov – not just a half-twist, but a full twist into the handstand.

Strelli

A difficult stunt in which a handstand is reached from a backwards roll. The move begins with a powerful forward swing down from a high angle. As the body passes between the bars, they are gripped in upper arm support. The body arches to help provide the exceptional momentum required to swing the body right up between the bars. At the crucial moment – and timing, as in many advanced stunts, is absolutely vital – the gymnast releases his upper arm grip, regrasps the bars in support and stretches his arms. If all has gone well, he will be in a handstand, and if it has gone perfectly, he will be able to halt the swing at the right instant to freeze the handstand.

Team gold medallist Igarashi (Japan) at the 1976 Games in a handstand that would be improved if the feet were better extended and the body straightened

10 The High Bar

This has always been reckoned the show-piece of the gymnastic scene, though many believe it has now been overtaken by the electrifying developments on the women's asymmetric bars. The horizontal bar, or high bar, as it is more popularly known, invites a short, spectacular exercise largely composed of swinging circles, the climax of which – the dismount – undoubtedly provides gymnastics with its most exciting moment. As the bar is itself more than eight feet (2.44 m) above the ground and the expert often leaves it while travelling upwards and outwards at high speed, the flight off can be really thrilling and extremely dangerous unless the gymnast is totally equipped technically for the precision of his departure and the force of his landing.

The high bar was the third of the creations of the 19th century German gymnastic dynamo, Jahn, whose other babies were the pommel horse and the parallel bars. It was then a massive wooden affair, $2\frac{1}{2}$ inches (63 mm) in diameter, and was used, as were all Jahn's developments, as much to demonstrate strength as swing. Even as late as the early 20th century, competitors were required to demonstrate strength on the high bar, but by then the rings, which had also been in existence for a hundred years, were beginning to take over the muscular aspect of the exercise. Thereafter, bar work developed exclusively towards swinging movements, and now a competitor is not permitted to perform any move on the bar that can be accomplished by strength alone.

For perfection on the high bar you need look no further than Mitsuo Tsukahara of Japan, winner of the event at both the Munich and Montreal Olympics

It is the ideal apparatus, really the only one, for the man with a comparatively low strength/weight ratio.

The world's first horizontal bar was no doubt a convenient tree branch, and the action of swinging in a long hang, or full extension, is such a natural one if you just look at the apes, that it is unthinkable that there was ever a time when young men did not use some handy bar for swinging exercise. But Jahn it was who regularized the activity and had the apparatus constructed on which it could best be done. Now that it has been refined, the bar is of steel just over an inch thick, nearly eight feet (2.44m) long and mounted on posts 8 feet 2½ inches (2.5 m) high. Each post is securely braced by two wire struts anchored to the floor, and a large area on each side of the bar is covered with thick matting. The exercise must be both vigorous and continuous, and as well as full extension circles, known as giant swings, or wheels, it must include circles in the support position, twists, changes of grip and, to qualify for top marks in an advanced competition, one move in which the gymnast first releases and then regrasps the bar with both hands at the same time.

Depending on the direction of the movement that follows, the bar is held in a regular grip, palms facing forward, knuckles between the gymnast and the bar, or a reverse grip, palms facing the gymnast, on the other side of the bar. In the United States these are better known as overgrip and undergrip, and the importance of using the correct one soon becomes obvious to the gymnast. It is, for instance, highly dangerous to make a vigorous forward swing in the hang position when using a reverse grip, because the hands could not prevent the body from flying off the bar. One of the early skills that a coach will try to teach the novice is the facility of swiftly changing grip – and knowing when to do it.

Though a great deal of variety can be achieved in the disposition of the body, there are basically only two ways in which the gymnast can hold himself on the high bar: in hang, when his body is under the bar; and in support, when it is largely over it. Though you will never see it still, the standard front hang is the most common of all positions: the body hanging perfectly straight under the bar like a pendulum, legs together, toes pointed, head between arms. The advanced gymnast differentiates between an active hang in this position, when the muscles of his body are tightened ready for a physical effort he is about to make, and a passive hang when he is totally relaxed in the course of a swing. The gymnast will often be seen in a front hang with bent arms – that is, with his chin pulled up level with the bar; and in a bent inverted hang, with his arms straight and his legs tightly piked at the hips, so that they pass between his arms and are parallel to the ground – a position already seen on the parallel bars. He may hang with one knee hooked over the bar, and he may hang totally inverted, head down. The latter is most frequently seen with one leg on each side of the bar, during a stride circle.

The support positions are never seen statically, which they are, almost, on the parallel bars and pommel horse; but they are exactly similar and are frequently passed through in the course of high bar routines. In front support the arms are straight, shoulders above hands, which are in regular grip, the body is slightly arched and leans over the bar, pressing against it at the hips; the legs are straight and together. Back

12 High bar: Hecht dismount

support is seldom seen on the high bar, it is as though the gymnast had turned 180 degrees, so the bar is behind the seat, with the arms still straight and taking the weight of the body. It is not an easy position to attain. In stride support the arms take almost all the weight again, but the bar is under the upper thigh of the forward leg. The legs are widely split.

Swings

Nothing is more important than that the gymnast should learn to swing properly, a very smooth and satisfying movement. From straight swinging in regular grip, never rising above the horizontal, the beginner on the high bar can practise dismounts with a forward swing and those vital grip changes. On his forward swing he will turn his body on the side, change one hand to a reverse grip, putting him in what is called mixed grip, and then the other, so that by the time he is ready for the return swing he is facing the other way and is in regular grip. When that can be accomplished without problems, he will progress to making the full half turn and changing the grip with both hands at once. When starting in reverse grip, the changes must be made at the peak of the back swing, remembering that a full forward swing must never be made with the hands in reverse grip.

The swing in the bent inverted hang position is often used, and is a tricky one to master. The piking of the body begins at the top of the back swing, is at its tightest as the body passes the vertical, and opens to

The coach's eyes are on the grip, more vital in this event than any other. Using the reverse grip, this gymnast is descending in a backward giant wheel

Reverse grip again as Stan Wild (GB) hovers high over the bar. Once the bar was 2½ inches (6.25 cm) thick and made of wood. Now of steel, it is just over one inch (2.5 cm)

13 High bar: giant circle, or wheel

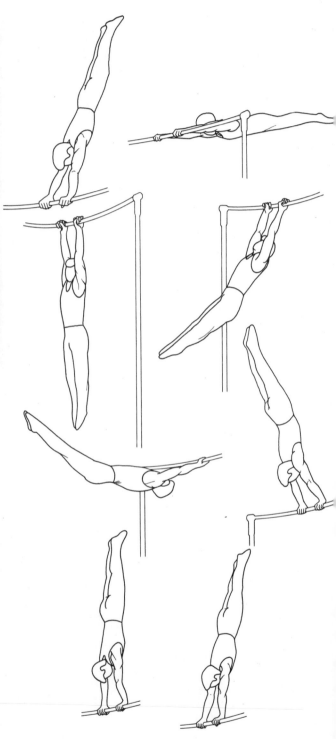

about 90 degrees at the top of the forward swing. This remains the pattern of the swinging, both forward and backward, and many gymnasts find it difficult to get into the rhythm of opening and closing the body, without which little height is achieved on the swings.

In his basic training, the gymnast will be required to work on many techniques that will get him from a support to a hanging position, and vice versa, and the more varied his repertoire, the more fluent his routine will eventually become. Of the kips, the most commonly seen takes the gymnast from a front hang swing to a front support.

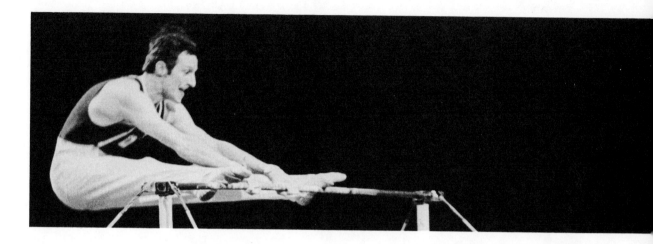

Wild grits his teeth for a sole circle, in which the performer revolves with his feet pressed firmly against the bar and hands in regular or overgrip

On the second half of his forward swing, the performer extends his body completely, then quickly lifts his straight legs so that the ankles and, if the swing has been strong enough, the knees, reach the bar. He lifts his hips, keeping the bar against his legs, closing the angle between arms and body. The body meanwhile is swinging back, but because the gymnast is pressing down on the bar with his hands and arms, the hips rise round it into the front support and on, perhaps, to a layout or handstand. Many performers change their grip to reverse when the forward swing ends.

Front hang to back support, which is probably more often seen on the women's asymmetric bars than on the high bar, is achieved by moving from a forward swing into the bent inverted hang swing. On the latter half of the backward swing in this position, the gymnast raises his legs vertically against the bar. As he pulls against it the momentum of the swing takes him on top of the bar and into back support.

Circles

There is hardly a trick in the gymnast's book that is not designed to join one circle to another. Circles are the flesh and blood of the high bar routine, short ones and long ones, bent ones and straight ones, and in assembling his optional programme (not an easy matter, if only because of the vast range of material available compared to the rest of the men's apparatus) the gymnast is chiefly concerned with a pattern of ever-changing circles. Sometimes he revolves tightly to the bar in front or back hip circles, also known as support turns.

For a back hip circle, the gymnast swings the legs back from a front support position to lift the body clear of the bar. When they swing forward again, the performer wraps himself in a pike round the bar, at the same time lifting his head and throwing his shoulders backwards. The body revolves quite fast, and he has to make a positive effort to hold the bar into his hips. The front hip circle does not have the benefit of that initial leg swing, and the impetus for the rotation comes from the gymnast bending at the hips as he falls forward. The back hip

One of Britain's best high bar operators, Tommy Wilson, suffering in the Montreal Olympics. Despite the brevity of the exercise, the strain is immense

circle can also be performed, by the more experienced, as a free or floating circle, in which the bar is not held to the body. The arms remain straight, or very slightly bent, and as the body drops from its opening horizontal position it pikes slightly and is thrust by the hips up beyond the bar. The arms help the pull up and over, and the hand grip is adjusted (not changed) when the performer returns above the bar again.

Front and back seat circles begin in back support, with the bar behind the hips. For the back circle, the gymnast leans back, tightly pikes his legs and allows his seat to swing off the bar, so that he drops in a bent inverted hang swing. As that swing passes the vertical, the pike is opened and the hands press on the bar to bring the body into support again. A front seat circle is not for the novice: from back support, the gymnast lifts his hips off the bar, bending his upper body forward and dropping into a bent inverted hang – this time with the feet and head leading, not the seat. As soon as he passes the vertical, he opens the hips and pulls strongly on the bar so that the legs pass up and over it.

A stride support position is the opening for the circle often seen on the women's bars, where it is called a mill circle. With his hands in either mixed or reverse grip, and his legs well split over the bar, the gymnast falls forward, keeping his arms straight. The move needs to be swift, with the bar held under the upper thigh of the leading leg. This circle should be performed with the hands in reverse grip.

The goal of all gymnasts on the high bar is to perform the wheel (or giant circle, or giant swing) – complete revolutions of the bar with arms outstretched and body extended, when up to five times the force of gravity may be exerted on the performer's shoulders. Most are encouraged to master the half giant first, a useful step not

Changing grip is an important facet of work on the high bar. Here Andrianov's undergrip for the back uprise is about to change for his forward descent

difficult to reach if the gymnast is already performing good hang swings. It should take him through about 270 degrees, starting with a good high layout from the front support position and swinging with full amplitude right round to the horizontal and beyond.

The full wheel is said to proceed from handstand to handstand, either forward or backwards, but in fact on the high bar there is no such thing as a handstand – just a move that passes through the handstand position. Though to the spectator the body usually appears to be fully extended during a wheel, the sharpest eyes will see that while the drop from the apex of the movement, whether backwards or forwards, begins at full stretch, there is a change in the attitude of the body near the bottom of the swing. In the backward wheel, the body begins to arch as it drops near the vertical, and the feet lead the body into the beginning of the rise; before the horizontal is reached, the back is rounded and the hips take over the lead. In a forward wheel, the body remains extended throughout the drop from top to bottom, but as soon as the vertical is passed the feet lead the rise and the body maintains a slight pike until the last 45 degrees of the circle.

Among the splendid variations to the wheel introduced by the really expert, the twist to handstand is one of the most popular. Again, the word handstand should not be taken too literally. When the horizontal has been passed in the upswing, the performer releases one hand, twists his body and regrasps. In the backward circle, it is the shoulders that begin the twist, and when it is completed, the grip must be changed to regular if the revolution is to proceed; in the forward circle, the feet and hips are the first to twist, and the grip changes to reverse.

Three moves incorporating both the giant swing and the bent inverted hang are only seen in the highest class of gymnastics, but deserve detailed attention. The inverted giant swing can be inserted into a backward wheel: on the upswing, the arch of the body is maintained all the way up to the handstand position. Immediately that is reached, and as the body begins to fall, the legs are bent at the hips and passed between the arms in the tightest of pikes, nose to knees. The momentum of the swing must take the body, with the back still rounded and parallel to the ground, way up above the bar, when the hips are thrust up further and the legs extended again ready for another backward circle.

The Stalder was named after its creator, a Swiss gymnast who failed by only five-hundredths of a point to win the high bar gold medal for the second time in 1952. It must be performed at great speed, to provide the power necessary to complete the movement. It begins on the upswing of a forward wheel. As usual, the legs lead the swing, and as the body rises through the horizontal, they go on bending at the hips to reach an angle with the body of 90 degrees or less. As the body reaches the top of its wheel, the legs are straddled. The swing down commences and the legs, now outside the arms, pike more tightly to avoid hitting the bar. The ankles almost touch it as the hips drop to the bottom of the circle and the legs are folded absolutely flat down outside the shoulders. On the swing goes, led by the seat. As that rises above the bar, the pike unfolds and the straddle narrows for the handstand position.

You might not think that anyone would wish to create anything more difficult than that while he is whirling round the high bar, but in the Olympics of 1964 (the year of the Yamashita vault) the gymnastic world saw such a high bar stunt performed by Yukio Endo, who won not the bar but the all-round individual championship. It is a Stalder backwards, and in the sport's official jargon is described as a backwards swing uprise to a handstand to a backwards floating hip circle with a straddle to a handstand. Most people prefer to call it an Endo.

The performer might be concluding a backward wheel, arches his body as it rises to the peak, and at the handstand position straddles his legs and begins to pike. Rapidly, the straddle gets as wide as possible and the pike as tight as possible, so that by the time the feet are leading the swing under the bar the gymnast's head and shoulders have emerged above the back of his knees. This total fold of the body, for which phenomenal flexibility of the hips is

Hiroshi Kajiyama tucking into a backward somersault as he leaves the bar. The height and speed of such dismounts makes landing a matter of some violence

essential, must be maintained until the body has risen above the bar, when the pike unfolds and the straddle closes to the handstand.

Dismounts

You might think that if you can perform a good Stalder or an Endo in a routine that may last no more than 15 seconds, you are made. In fact, as suggested earlier, the importance of the dismount almost certainly outweighs any other movement that may be demonstrated. In its simpler versions, the gymnast may dismount from a forward or backward hang swing, with a good stretch on the flight off; or from front support into an underswing, in which he begins as though he were doing a backward hip circle and then thrusts the hips and chest up and out for an arched flight off; and either of those can be complicated by a half turn in flight. Perhaps from front support he will swing his legs back and up and go over the bar in a squat or straddle, as though vaulting.

Any of those make most acceptable elementary dismounts, but as his confidence and technical skill increase, the gymnast will be looking for something more spectacular. The backward somersault is certainly that: from a really strong forward swing, probably following a wheel, the gymnast pushes on the bar from his shoulders just before releasing at the horizontal, to provide a high upward 'float'. The body should remain smoothly arched throughout the somersault, with the motivation for the turn being provided by the hips and shoulders, and not the legs. The arms spread for the swallow flight before the legs drop to the landing spot.

A prodigious upward swing of the hips as the gymnast leaves the bar, with knees already bending, leads to the double backward tucked somersault dismount, a marvellous sight in which the greatest performers achieve enormous height on the first somersault. The basic 'straight body' somersault dismount can be enhanced with a twist; or the move can be performed in a tucked or bent body (half piked) position.

You may remember the Hecht and giant Hecht vaults. There is also a Hecht high bar dismount that shows off the typical 'winged float' position to its best advantage. It is produced after a backward wheel, at the conclusion of which the gymnast is not fully extended, but has let his body fall slightly behind his arms. This allows him the extra impetus at the top of the downswing caused by the legs catching up, and power on the downswing is vital. As he passes through the bottom of the circle (for the second time), the hips are leading the swing and the head is forward on to the chest. On the upswing, the performer pulls hard down on the bar, causing the legs to swing up and the shoulders to sink. At this moment, as Kaneko so graphically puts it, 'your chest muscles are stretched almost to the point of tearing'. On that upswing, then, the body has passed from a slight pike to an arch, and as the force of that pull on the bar (remember, the hands are in reverse grip) sends the whole body high above it, the forward momentum of the wheel gives the body forward flight, with the bar released. The body is arched, the arms fully extended sideways, and down from ten or twelve feet the performer flies gracefully in for his landing. The operation is equally impressive when performed with a straddle, which was the compulsory dismount at the Montreal Olympics.

11 Asymmetric Bars

Many people say the man's high bar is the most exciting piece of gymnastic apparatus. It used to be so, but for many others the superb talents and electrifying courage of artists like Korbut and Comaneci has changed that. There is now nothing more thrilling in the Olympic programme than the few seconds in which the world's greatest female gymnasts are working on the asymmetric bars, or the high-and-low bars, or the uneven parallel bars, or what we shall from now on call simply 'the uneven bars'. In terms purely of its physical demands, it is the hardest of all the exercises – the least 'feminine'. The floor requires grace, agility and vigour, the vault adds speed, the beam replaces vigour with balance; the uneven bars require a measure of all those, plus the unique requirement of strength – a quality which women do not acquire naturally, particularly in the arms and shoulders. It is a hard, bruising exercise, turning soft hands into calloused ones and punishing the groin and the front of the the thighs by sheer vicious contact with the equipment. Nowhere in the men's programme does anything like that happen.

Until about 40 years ago, women used to use the parallel bars for training and exercise, but not as a competitive exercise. This was discouraged when the move was intensified to take the muscle out of their side of the sport, and somebody, it is extremely difficult to establish just who, had the brilliant idea of monkeying about with the parallel bars on their behalf. It was an extraordinary thing to do, quite illogical, entirely without precedent. They preserved exactly the shape and diameter of the bar, and the length, and more or less the width between them, though this is adjustable to suit the gymnast; but they pushed one bar down to less than 5 feet (1.5 m) and pulled the other one up to 7 feet 6 inches (2.3 m). It would have been very interesting to see what the gymnasts of the 1930s made of the new equipment, how they tackled the weird object. By 1936 it was firmly enough established to be demonstrated at the Berlin Olympic Games, and when the women's individual competition was introduced at the Helsinki Games of 1952, the uneven bars were there.

Their exploitation owes little to parallel bars technique and almost everything to intelligent adaptation of skills developed on the men's high bar. The exercise must be a combination of ceaseless swinging and circling, flight from one bar to the other, twisting, turning and springing. Pauses must be imperceptible. No 'held' positions are allowed, so even the handstand on the top bar should not be static, but part of a circle the speed of which decreases so much that the judges can admire the performer's control and balance. As much in this exercise as on the men's pommel horse, it is important for the gymnast from the start to get in the habit of linking one stunt with the next in a smooth, swift flow. Agility, flexibility, strength – without these qualities a girl can hardly approach the uneven bars; and for her to succeed in the sort of programme that wins competitions, for her to

One of the most famous sights in gymnastics – Olga Korbut poised illogically over the top bar. It is the superb arch of the body that preserves balance

Another slice of perfection from Korbut. Note the mechanism by which gymnasts can adjust the distance between high and low bars to suit their own height

be able to attempt the notorious dislocation catch, she must also have built up an impressive store of confidence and courage.

It is no good pretending that the novice can tackle the bars without some suffering. Initially, it will be to the hands, unless she is blessed with remarkably tough ones. The incessant, high-speed rubbing of palms on bars is almost certain to lead to sore and blistered hands. The beginner is doubly susceptible, not only because her hands are unused to such punishment, but because it will be some time before she learns when to grip tight and when to release; meanwhile she tends to try to grip all the time. The use of leather hand grips for bar work does not necessarily prevent blisters, but it does delay them. Further comfort, and safety, is provided by gymnastic chalk (magnesium carbonate), which absorbs perspiration and so helps to stop the hands slipping.

In due course the surface of the hands will harden and blisters will no longer be a problem. The next hazard is callouses, which may not be a handicap in the gym, but are socially unwelcome to most females. These lumps of hard skin can be gently rubbed away with a pumice stone, but the regular application of lanolin cream may prevent them forming. You will notice, incidentally, that no experienced gymnast, however resistant her hands have become, goes to the bars without chalk and hand grips. Nor will she start work until she has checked the security of the apparatus (except in competition, where it is permanently supervised) and the distance between the bars. This width can be altered by two simple screw adjustments, and is set by the gymnast or her coach to that precise distance that suits her height and reach. Finally, before mounting the bars, the gymnast will want to make sure the whole of her landing area is adequately protected by mats, and possibly by a crash mat if she is working on a particularly difficult stunt.

Even in competition, the gymnast who

The unique and hair-raising Nadia Comaneci version of the Radochla somersault, in which she straddle-somersaults from the high bar and returns to it

wants to start her routine with a high bounce may use a springboard to get her there. It will immediately be removed by her coach, or a spotter. The beginner will not want to do anything of the kind: most of the basic elements of an uneven bars exercise can be practised initially on a single bar, and where possible this should be the low one – or better still, a single horizontal bar set low, or one of a pair of men's parallel bars with its partner removed. There is no point in a girl who is facing for the first time the rather daunting business of whirling her body round a bar, having to do so with the added worry of nearby obstacles or extreme height.

There is more than one way of gripping the bar, and the performer's grip must change to suit the movement. In competition, it is essential to demonstrate grip changes. The normal, regular, or overgrip is achieved by facing the bar and laying the hands on it: the thumbs are beside the forefingers, the knuckles between the gymnast and the bar. The other two most common grips are the reverse, in which the hands pass under the bar to grip it from the far side; and the mixed – one of each.

Basic positions are the same as those on the men's high bar: front support, in which the extended body rests against the bar at the hips, supported by straight arms. The shoulders are above and slightly in front of the hands, the head is held up and back, and there is a slight arch to the back. In back support, the body leans slightly backwards over the bar, which is at the seat. Again, the straight arms, which are close to the hips, take most of the weight. Sometimes the legs are raised and the upper body held upright. Stride support is an easy position to hold, but not to get into: one leg is either side of the bar and well split, the weight taken on the hands and the upper thigh of the forward leg. This is the position from which the popular mill circle is made.

The two hang positions that occur most frequently through routines are the long hang and the piked hang, which is also known as the half-inverted hang or the bent inverted hip hang. The long hang is almost

British expert Barbara Slater in her graceful Hecht dismount. Like the vault of the same name, it is characterized by the 'swallow' attitude in flight

too obvious to mention – the gymnast hangs at full stretch from the high bar – but for the fine distinction between a passive hang and an active hang. Expert performers allow the body to relax into a passive hang as often as possible when they are swinging, because it lowers the centre of gravity and produces a longer, smoother swing. They move to the active hang in preparation for a new movement, by tightening the relevant muscles from shoulders to hips.

The swing from a long hang is probably seen more often than any other single movement in a routine. It takes the gymnast from bar to bar and into the various beats and wraps that, at high speed, contribute so much to the excitement on the uneven bars. Clearly, the low bar is soon going to obstruct the forward swing. The performer should hit it at groin level, just below the hip bone. To that end, she adjusts the distance between the bars; girls too short to achieve that ideal, who hit the low bar lower down the thighs, should not attempt the

long swing. To lessen the impact – and from all points of view she should certainly aim to lessen it – she swings with an arched back, and on impact lets her legs swing on. This takes the body into a pike with the low bar nestling in the pit of the stomach, a position known as a wrap. At the end of it the legs swing down again and at the same time the stomach helps the body push back off the bar, returning it to a long swing. As anybody who has watched uneven bars work will know, the bars have very considerable flexibility. This not only softens the blow when you hit them, but gives punch to the rebound.

The piked hang is often seen in the course of other movements, and is no problem to achieve. From the long hang, the gymnast raises the legs from the hips and lifts the hips themselves, until the legs are between her arms and parallel to the floor. It is the position of the hips that governs the stability of this hang: if they are too high, the head tends to drop and the body to roll on backwards; if not high enough, it is difficult for the gymnast to stop the pike falling back to a hang.

It takes a lot of practice to master the business of swinging in the piked hang. At the top of the forward swing, the body must be tightly piked, with the hips high above the level of the bar and the head vertically downwards. As the body rises to the top of the backward swing, the legs open almost to a right angle; at its peak, the head is at bar level. This swing can be accomplished on either bar.

So can the underswing, another useful basic element, which has the advantage of being easy for beginners to practise on the low bar. Known also as the float, it should begin with the gymnast standing arms' length from the bar. She springs into a take-off in which her hips rise vertically, so that as she grasps the bar, her arms and back should form a straight line. There needs to be a good thrust from the ground or off a board, so that the body has the greatest possible distance in which to swing forward. The pike unfolds during the forward swing, so the feet just clear the floor and the body opens right out to full extension. While she is practising, the young gymnast can release at the extent of the swing to land on her feet, or can swing back again, keeping the legs straight, to repeat it, perhaps gaining enough impetus on the back swing to rise to a layout position, the body flying well above the bar.

The underswing can also lead to two other basic moves of slightly greater difficulty, the upstart and the underswing with half turn. To achieve the latter, the gymnast swings forward with an extra lift to the hips and legs, and a positive pull on the bar. As the swing rises to its peak, she lets go with one hand and turns her shoulders over, regrasping the bar in mixed grip. It is not a difficult move to perform, but it is difficult

14 Asymmetric bars: mill circle

to perform it perfectly, with the timing of the rise and turn precisely coordinated.

Upstarts

The upstart can be worked on either bar, and from a variety of starting positions. It takes the gymnast from under the bar, in some form of hang, to over the bar, in support. Moving to it from the underswing on the low bar, the performer lets the extended forward swing turn into a pike, the toes reaching back to the bar and then moving up higher, thrust up by the hips until the knees have passed the bar. From that peak the pike unfolds with a strong swing as the shoulders and hips rise, the hands pressing down on the bar to take the body up to a front support – and on, if wanted, to a layout. From the same long underswing, the pike can take the feet between the arms and under the bar, rising on the other side so that the bar passes down the back of the thighs until the gymnast is sitting on the bar in back support.

There is a difference in British and American terminology that crops up right across gymnastics, but nowhere is it more confusing than in this event. What the British call an upstart is usually known in America as an uprise, a much more agreeable term. But the British use uprise to describe something else: an upstart that begins where it will end, in support above the bar. And Americans describe as a kip a move that most British call an upstart between bars. This, often seen, begins with the gymnast's seat resting on the low bar with the body entirely straight and the hands grasping the high bar – what some British coaches call a back support position, and some a back lying position.

You can see that, because of this starting position, no forward swing is possible to give impetus to the backward swing and rise to front support. It is replaced by swinging the legs suddenly downwards and at the same time extending the shoulders forwards, and then rapidly swinging the legs up, to bring the ankles to the high bar. The same powerful move continues with the hips thrusting up and the legs urgently rising even higher, lightly touching the high bar. At the same time that the gymnast is forcing her legs into this rise, her body will have begun to swing backwards, because the seat is no longer in contact with the low bar. Keeping her arms straight as long as possible, she presses the bar to her legs and pulls on it to complete the circling rise of the upper body over the bar into front support.

Circles

With an understanding of those few basic positions and linking moves, it is time to look at the heart of the uneven bars operation: circles. You can hardly watch two seconds of Comaneci without seeing a circle, a complete rotation of one of the bars, and it would take full concentration to count the number of circles she performs in the course of a routine.

We mentioned the mill circle earlier. From straddle support on either bar, the gymnast lifts her body off the bar, taking the weight on her hands. The forward leg stretches well out and the hips and upper body lean forward with it, the head held high. The circle is swift, the legs kept perfectly straight and well split. Ideally, as the body whizzes round, the angles between the legs and between each leg and the upper body should be equal. Based on the same technique is the backwards knee circle, in which the gymnast starts in straddle support and moves back so that the bar is hooked under the knee of her forward leg. Much depends on the upward swing of the free leg.

Hip circles start from the normal front support position in forward grip. For the backward circle, the legs swing forward then back into a layout, with the whole body horizontal and the arms straight, shoulders over the bar. As the body drops into the swing, it remains absolutely straight but is

RIGHT: It was her performance on the uneven bars in 1976 that won for Comaneci the first 'perfect' score in Olympic history. Three times she achieved a maximum

BELOW: Another Hecht dismount, in which the body is rather too sharply arched and the gymnast may have found it difficult to achieve a stable, upright landing

Korbut reaching for the low bar during the 1975 World Cup in London. She won the all-round silver medal, but could not contest the individual events

pulled into the bar at the hips, revolving tightly around it and over it, led by the legs. A forward hip circle is achieved by falling forward from front support. This time the body is not kept straight, but is piked around the bar, which as ever remains tight to the hips. As the fall forward begins, it is important to drop the hands under the bar slightly ahead of the body rotation. This ensures that the big swing of the legs down and under the bar does not pull the body away from it. A popular progression from this circle, frequently used by advanced gymnasts, is the free forward circle of the low bar (that is, without the hands holding it) that is concluded by the outstretched hands grasping the high bar. On paper, the move seems to defy gravity, which is seldom a wise thing to do; in practice, it cannot commence from a static position, but from

a vigorous arrival over the low bar. The performer leads the circle with her arms, the body piked throughout, and the whole movement must be very fast.

The backward hip circle can be preceded by a swing in long hang to make a useful combination. Starting from front support on the high bar, the gymnast swings back to a layout and swings down, fully extended, to wrap around the low bar. At the instant that pike is completed, she lets go of the high bar and goes into a free backward hip circle, regrasping the low bar in front support. The danger exists, when a novice is trying this move, that she lets go on the high bar too soon, before the legs have gained sufficient upward impetus to take them on over the low bar. If an expert performer wants to make matters more difficult, she can go into the long swing with her back to the low bar, and put in a half-turn when the swing is at its fullest extent.

Seat circles tend to be more worrying

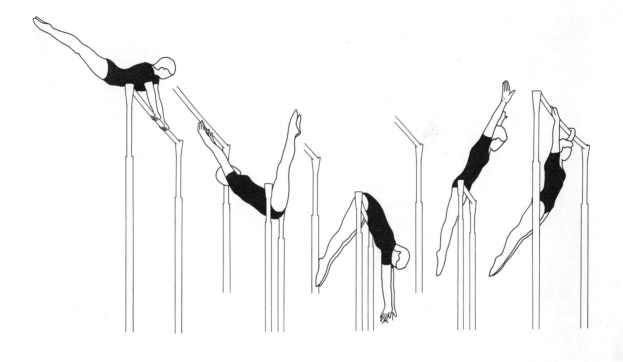

15 Asymmetric bars: dislocation catch

As the low bar is less than five feet (1.5 m) off the floor, hangs from it have to be piked or half-piked. Note the unusually heavy wrist protection in use

than hip circles to the beginner, because the bar is always behind her, but there is no other reason why they should not be simply accomplished. From a normal back support, the legs are piked vertically for a backward seat circle. The hips move out from the bar and the body drops backwards, led by the shoulders. As the body circles the bar, the hips close to it, the pike remains tight until the vertical has been passed. On the rise, the upper body opens up with the wrists quickly coming to the top of the bar and the back support position is reached

again. For a forward seat circle, the body remains piked throughout. From the opening back support, the gymnast falls forward, trying to achieve distance from the bar and keeping the arms straight. At the bottom of the circle, to which position the gymnast must not drop suddenly, the legs begin to open from their tight pike. With straight arms, the performer pulls on the bar to complete the rise and take the legs up over the bar again.

Sole circles are usually performed with the legs straddled and the feet on the bar outside the hands, though the reverse position can be used. The gymnast drops backwards, feet pressing into the bar and hands pulling strongly against it. On the rise, this can develop into a layout and dismount; or from the low bar, a release and regrasp on the high bar, which can include a half-turn in the air. With a reverse grip on the bar, a forward sole circle can similarly be achieved.

Still included among the circles, though it is a more advanced stunt than any of those yet mentioned, is the dislocation catch, a spectacular item. From a layout on the high bar the gymnast goes into a long swing and backward hip circle on the low bar, but this time after releasing her grasp on the high bar, she does not regrasp on the low. The backward circle is executed with the body well piked, as before, but when the performer has reached what would normally have been the front support position on the low bar, her arms are widespread above her head and turned out, with the fingers beginning to point at the high bar behind her. At that instant, if the movement is frozen by the camera, her position seems impossible – there is nothing to stop her sliding to the ground. But the back has changed its atti-

tude and is now hollow, with the hips thrusting hard onto the low bar. The rotation of the legs has been sharply checked, which contributes to the thrust, and the whole body springs backwards in arched flight. The gymnast cannot see where she is going, but sufficient practice with her coach will have taught her that those wing-like arms and hands (some call it the eagle grip) are going to catch the high bar. This is so splendid a move that, in top-class competition, one longs to see it performed again in slow motion. Alas, it is all so fast that one blink will cause the spectator to miss the vital moment.

Somersaults

You might not think it possible that a gymnast could somersault on the uneven bars and regain her hold until you see it done. These days, it is frequently done by the experts, either in one of its so-called simpler forms like the tumble turn or, by the very best, in what is known as a Radochla, after its creator, Bridgette Radochla of the German Democratic Republic.

The tumble turn does not have the sort of flight that causes one to gasp at floor exercise somersaults, because it happens between bars. From a strong back swing in long hang, the performer pulls herself into a very tight pike with the legs spread wide in a straddle. At the same time she closes the angle between arms and body. All that is done very quickly, so that as she swings forward she is head down and folded in two. At the instant the forward swing takes her head and shoulders above the low bar, she releases her grip on the high bar. The rotation of the body continues, with the hips dropping, the hands reaching for the low bar and the feet pointing under it. From there she will probably go into an underswing and upstart.

The Radochla more or less reverses that procedure, which is at least twice as difficult and twice as dangerous and a crash mat is strongly advised during training. From front support on the low bar, with her back to the high bar, the gymnast swings her legs forward and urgently back, as if to go into

RIGHT: Another view of the devastating Comaneci Radochla, that impressed the Montreal judges just as much as the public. Infallibly, she feels for the top bar

BELOW: East German Annelore Zinke in a standard Radochla. Surprisingly, she beat Korbut for the world uneven bars title in 1974, but was not in the Olympic team

a layout. But the legs are straddled, and pike as the hips rise high. As they come to the peak of the swing, she lets go of the low bar and reaches between her legs for the high bar. The legs must be kept tightly piked during the somersault, opening out and swinging down after the catch, to take the body to front support on the high bar.

Gymnastics being, as we have said before, a business in which the best performers are constantly striving to outdo their rivals in the creation of difficulty, it was inevitable that one day someone would go one further than Radochla. Not surprisingly, it was Nadia Comaneci, who took off from the high bar in similar fashion and performed a straddle somersault high in the air, returning to the high bar. It was one of those days when seeing was hardly believing.

Dismounts

Dismounts from all apparatus are vastly important, and none gives greater scope for showmanship than the men's high bar and the women's uneven bars. In the early stages, the gymnast goes for a nice, clean underswing dismount from the low, and later the high, bar; or for flank dismounts from the low bar, or a good backward swing through a layout. Perhaps next she will try squat and straddle dismounts over the bar from front support, concentrating on a well-extended and slightly arched body in the flight off the bar. But once she has mastered her basic training on the bars, she will be looking for something more exciting.

A handstand off, using both bars, always provokes admiration. From a front support on the high bar, the performer reaches down with one hand to grasp the low bar, first bending tightly at the hips and then swinging the legs powerfully up into the handstand. As soon as this is accomplished, with one hand on each bar, the high bar hand pushes off, sending the shoulders into a quarter-turn, pivoting on the low bar hand. The initial swing of the legs over the high bar must be strong enough for the movement to take the legs over the handstand and smoothly to the ground, which the gymnast reaches facing the bars.

Among the advanced dismounts, the one most often seen is probably the Hecht, also the name given to a vault in which the gymnast makes a long, horizontal flight. In its complete version, it is preceded by a long swing and free backward hip circle, just as if it were leading to a dislocation catch. The body swings off the high bar, pikes round the low and remains piked until shortly before the moment the gymnast would be taking off backwards for the catch. At that point she thrusts strongly against the bar with her thighs and reaches forward and up with her arms and upper body. In theory, that combined with the forward movement inspired by the long swing, is enough to lift the body above the low bar and send it well forward for a landing. In practice, there is likely to be quite a long period of painful gym work while the gymnast finds her legs are not rising enough to clear the bar; and having got over that problem by thrusting even more urgently against the bar, she finds she has projected herself into a nose dive towards the mat. When she achieves the necessary lift both of the chest and the legs, and has sufficient forward momentum for a good post-flight and upright landing, there are few more satisfying or more effective moves on the uneven bars than the Hecht.

12 The Balance Beam

There is something extraordinary about the balance beam. Ask any inactive spectator what is the easiest piece of equipment in the Olympic programme, and he will almost certainly tell you it must be the beam. Ask any female competitor what is the hardest of her four events, and almost certainly she will give the same answer: the beam. All right, the spectator may say, to get a high score in senior competitions you have to do impossible things like free walkovers and flic-flacs, but mostly it is just walking up and down and turning and jumping a bit. Anybody should be able to cope with that, he says, and he cannot understand why so many girls fall off (half a mark deducted immediately, and you only have ten seconds to get on again). What's the problem?

Getting on is the first problem, and sometimes a gymnast will never really recover from an unstable mount. It sets up a dose of jitters and for the rest of the time something is fluttering away inside her. The beam is not exactly a tightrope, but it is only four inches (10 cm) wide which is just about the width of a competitor's foot and it is nearly four feet (1.2 m) high, at least chest high to most girls. A heave and a scramble will not win many friends, nor points, so how do you spring lightly to your feet up there? Nowhere else in the whole field of gymnastics does the performer have trouble before she even starts her exercise.

Once she is up, what next? Walking along the beam should not be too much trouble, if she takes it gingerly; and no doubt the spectator would say he could run along if

he held his breath and did it quickly and jumped off at the other end. But to run along with his head held high, a hop in the middle, and at the end a full turn into a knees bend? That would finish him, never mind the handstands and backward rolls. The minute and a half that a gymnast must spend prancing, dancing, twisting and tumbling on the beam (precisely, between 75 and 95 seconds) is the most exacting time of her competitive life.

Fortunately, it is the least physically demanding exercise, the least tiring, so from that point of view at any rate, there is almost no limit to the amount of practice time a gymnast can spend on the beam. Certainly no other gymnastic discipline needs more practice. There will always be enthusiastic gymnasts who never become agile or dexterous enough to perform the most breathtaking of the beam tricks, but one can truly say that the more time a youngster spends on the beam, the better she is quite certain to be. Absolute familiarity with that 16-foot (4.9 m) ribbon of airborne territory and the sensations it produces is the only basis on which confidence can be based. Without such confidence, skills are useless; even with it, the degree of concentration necessary is a considerable burden. On that critical matter balances the success of the operation: how to look happy and move lightly without relaxing the mental grip; how to concentrate unflaggingly and still enjoy it. There is no magic formula to guarantee that, but the young gymnast will be moving towards it when she is no more worried on

Composite picture puzzle: Munich Olympian
Yvonne Mugridge (GB) in a beam walkover.
Forward or backward? Take it from right to left

the beam than she is running up and down
her staircase at home.

Ernestine Carter has said that the beam,
at its best, requires 'the skill of a tightrope
walker, the grace of a ballerina and the
agility of an acrobat.' It is the most feminine
of all a woman's gymnastic efforts – and
feels particularly so because men do nothing
to compare with it. Nowhere else in the
gymnastic arena does a woman look so perfectly a woman as when she is on the beam,
a stage on which her quality is exposed to

the most thorough scrutiny, elevated, un-
masked, unable to deceive the eye with the
speed of movement. It takes more than skill
and more than confidence to stand up there
and be devoured by thousands of eyes. If
one had to choose one quality above all
without which a girl could never become a
champion on the beam, it would be poise.

A good coach can usually spot beam
potential by the way a young gymnast performs on the floor. She will be required to
do nothing on the beam that she does not
do in her floor exercises, but she will have
to do them more precisely, allowing her

One of the barefooted brigade, East Germany's young Silvia Hindorff, echoes our cover picture with this beautifully-balanced scale on the four-inch (10 cm) beam

Static poses such as this one by the great Erika Zuchold (GDR) must be used sparingly and only to demonstrate balance. The exercise should be fluid

body not the faintest flourish that is not under perfect control. 'Think straight', coach Jill Coulton says, 'think straight and move straight.' There she has rung the bell. It is all very well to obey the dictum when you can see the beam in front of you, or even when you remain in contact with it during a backward roll; but just consider taking off in a free cartwheel or a backward somersault – the discipline required to land on that same four-inch (10 cm) strip must be almost superhuman.

The training of a novice for the beam is a patient, painstaking business. It begins on a four-inch (10 cm) line on the floor, or in the case of tumbling activities, on a narrow bench covered with mats; then it moves on to a very low beam. No coach is going to allow a gymnast to try handsprings or walk-overs even on a bench unless she can perform them perfectly on the floor mat; and he is not going to put a youngster up on the four-foot (1.2 m) beam even for straight-forward walking and running until she can do it confidently and accurately on the beam a few inches (centimetres) off the floor. You in the audience may not think the beam is particularly high, not high enough to instil any sense of fear; but it is the gymnast's feet that are at the height of the beam – her eyes and her sense of balance are more than twice that height, and that is why the nerves begin to jangle in all except the coolest of customers. However confident and experienced the performer is, the matter of maintaining perfect line and balance is one that in itself requires her unwavering concentration every time she mounts the beam. The

ABOVE: Another favourite Korbut exhibition that helped to win the Soviet spellbinder two silver medals and one gold on the beam in world and Olympic events

LEFT: A classic feat of concentration and poise by Olga Korbut, but above all one that shows the uncanny flexibility of the spine needed to beat the best

incredible agility skills with which the greatest gymnasts astonish their audience are no problem to them at all by the time they take them up on the beam. Up there, there would be no way they could cope with them if they were.

So, the embryo Comaneci learns to walk prettily, run daintily, pause, pose, squat, kneel and turn without any kind of fear that a mistake could be punished by pain. Watch them in a training class and you will see that, night after night, they will get no further than learning to turn in various positions, or standing on one leg and gently exercising the other, or letting the arms flow above and around them as they walk. Not until those

16 Balance beam: mount to handstand

Ludmilla Tourischeva never had the cheek of some of her rivals, but for serenity she was supreme. She was once world, Olympic and European beam champion

simple operations can be performed freely, with total confidence and absolute stability, is the novice invited to rise higher. Running parallel to those preparations, she will be practising on the padded bench some of the simpler tumbling skills that she already performs expertly on the floor.

There has to be a special tension about the body whenever it moves on the beam (tension, not tenseness). Whatever the limbs are doing, the trunk must be invisibly anchored to the beam, rather as though it were held down by one of those chains that anchor a vaulting horse to the floor. The more extreme and extravagant the gesture of arm or leg, the tighter the gymnast holds her body, not allowing it to be upset.

17 Balance beam: free cartwheel

It was Nadia Comaneci's absurdly brilliant free backward walkover on the beam in London in 1975 that first alerted the western world to her talent

Slackness of the hips or shoulders is a sure step towards disaster. They must always be steady, and when they turn, they should turn together – a twisted torso instantly loses stability, because its weight is unevenly distributed. The gymnast should, incidentally, travel along the beam at least six times in the course of her routine, which should be varied as much as possible in movements, direction and rhythm. Her moves must be in a continuous flow, broken only three times by pauses, or rather, poses, that do not last more than three seconds each. Judges are usually watching keenly for hesitation before or after what are called 'superior movements' (the difficult ones), and also immediately after the mount and before the dismount, which must be streamlined into the flowing routine. It is worth remembering the advice of one of the

18 Balance beam: forward walkover

A forward walkover of the simple kind, without which no performance is complete. The 16 feet (4.8 m) of the beam must be frequently covered with the maximum variety

wisest and most successful of British coaches, Pauline Prestidge: if, even in practice, the gymnast has to stand on the beam plucking up courage for the next move, she is not ready to attempt it.

Mounting

A mount should be so well-integrated into the routine that it appears to be part of the move that follows it. No experienced gymnast thinks of the mount as the means of getting up on the beam – to her it is the start of a forward roll, or a handstand, or whatever she has chosen to begin her performance. Novices are urged to take the same attitude, though they are likely to break themselves in rather more gently.

There are almost no rules about mounting. The gymnast can walk into it, run at

ABOVE: It may be no more comfortable than lying down on a broomstick, but Barbara Slater (GB) is caught by the camera looking as though she is ready for sleep

ABOVE LEFT: The skill of a tightrope walker and the grace of a ballerina are necessary qualities, and one other, here shown by Korbut – the agility of an acrobat

FAR LEFT: On the beam and the floor, the gymnast must be a bit of an exhibitionist. One of Korbut's priceless talents was to look so happy while she showed off

LEFT: Hungarian beam expert Monika Csaszar in a splendidly adventurous leap. Not difficult on the ground, but her organs of balance are ten feet (3 m) higher than that

it, or spring from a board. She can jump at it squarely with a squat or a straddle, for instance, take an oblique approach for a scissor mount, or start from the end of the beam and perhaps go into a forward roll. Whatever she does, the performance is marked, and timed, from the instant her feet leave the floor.

A scissor mount to what is called the riding position is a good one for the beginner, as it does not involve too high a jump. From an oblique run she places one hand on the beam, takes off on the further foot and swings the nearer leg up and over the beam. The take-off leg follows, and both hands support the performer as she sits, in side-saddle style. From that position she can comfortably move into a squat rise, or lie on the beam for a backward roll.

A single-leg squat has a similar approach but needs a stronger take-off, for the hips must rise high enough to allow the mount to be made on one bent leg; the same technique will take the gymnast through a mount to stride support, the legs well split on either side of the beam.

More conventional vaulting technique is used for the square-on mounts. From the springboard the gymnast puts both hands on the beam and lifts the hips as high as possible. For a squat, the feet arrive between the hands, with bent knees; for the straddle, a slightly more difficult balancing

Tourischeva's feet cling to the beam's surface in a skilful box splits as she conducts an advanced exercise in the principles of cantilevered balance

job, the legs spread wide and the feet are placed outside the hands. One up on that is the straddle over, in which the legs straddle and are held out horizontally, with all the weight taken on the hands.

Many of these comparatively simple mounts may be made more difficult, and more impressive, by performing them without using the hands on the beam. Indeed, there is something hugely impressive in the quite uncomplicated step-on mount when it is done without hands. It makes a fine start to the exercise to see a gymnast spring swiftly from the floor right on to a standing position on the beam and straight into another movement.

The forward roll from a mount is a popular start from the end of the beam. The

Another fine leap, this time from one of the United States girls, Diane Dunbar, who have recently taken their country so near the top of the world rankings

Though Olga Koval has never represented the USSR in Olympics, she did in the 1975 World Cup, where this dismount was seen (and the scale shown on our cover)

gymnast usually either takes a short run from the floor, or springs from a board. Both hands are on top of the beam, fingers down the side; the take-off is vigorous, lifting the hips high as the head tucks down between the arms. The roll starts at the back of the neck and passes right down the rounded back to the hips. As it does so, the arms reach forward and the momentum of the roll – this is a fast movement – takes the upper body upright. One foot has been brought close in to the seat and it is on this that the body rises. The move fails completely if the roll does not move smoothly and strongly into the stand, or a crouch if it is the starting position for the next move.

The mount to handstand is also often seen from the end of the beam, but this calls for a very confident gymnast. The vigour needed in take-off to carry the hips high above straight arms is difficult to control, and tends to overbalance the handstand. To counteract this, performers keep the body piked and the legs straddled until the hips are over the shoulders.

The assembly of the balance beam exercise will probably include as many of the basic floor tumbling skills as the gymnast can smoothly and confidently incorporate – rolls, cartwheels, walkovers, tinsicas, back-flips. They have been discussed in detail earlier in the book, and the technique for performing them on the beam remains basically the same.

The need for absolute precision, however, cannot be too strongly emphasized. On the floor, any movement that passes through a handstand does so with the hands a secure shoulder's width apart. This enables the gymnast to maintain balance despite a deviation in the path the legs may take through the air. On the beam, the base over which the body is rotating is minute, and unless the feet pass directly over the hands in all such movement, there will be little chance of retaining balance. The back flip, or, even more appalling to contemplate, the back somersault, seems sheer madness on this tiny floor space, but as we know, they can be done by those whose technique is perfect and whose nerve and courage is supreme. When Nadia Comaneci, probably the finest beam artist ever known, first came to London in April 1975, those of us who saw her perform a free walkover were transfixed. It did not seem humanly possible to accomplish such a move on the beam, but it shows what the human body is capable of achieving with sufficient dedication – and sufficient practice. Even the compulsory exercise in the Olympics the following year, which needless to say, Comaneci won, required a one-armed cartwheel.

These exotic demonstrations, however, are for the masters of the sport, and even for them they occupy much less of their time on the beam than do the more mundane movements. The compulsories are packed with ballet stands, turns, spins, squats, balances and jumps, and it is a foolish gymnast who fails to perfect that side of her business before polishing the acrobatics. Static balances, of which only three may be held, are among the most beautiful moments of gymnastics, and can include positions that show not merely balance, but flexibility (splits and bridges) and strength (handstands). One of the abiding memories in recent gymnastic history must be Olga Korbut's fantastic box splits on the beam, legs seemingly cemented to its surface, that tiny torso arched back, arms and fingers exquisitely extended, the mischievous little face tilted back in triumph.

Jumps, which may be static or mobile, are highly favoured by the judges and most gymnasts devote much time to their practice. They aim to achieve the maximum height and yet to land softly, almost certainly with some leg action in the air, like a tuck or a scissors. Favourite of all, for those who are confident enough to perform it, is the stag jump, the leap that has length as well as height and passes through a splits at its peak.

Turning is probably the most difficult of all the basic skills of the beam and at the Montreal Olympics competitors had to demonstrate sixteen turns in the compulsory programme, one of which was a full 360 degree turn. You may be asked to make turns from every conceivable position – standing, squatting, sitting, kneeling, on one foot or two. The experts are agreed that the key to the technique is that the centre of gravity must be kept accurately over the exact point of turn, which is usually the ball of the foot. This is not as easy as it sounds, since at the time of the turn the body is often in an asymmetrical posture. The armchair reader can soon see the problem by standing up for a moment: with one foot flat on the floor, as it might briefly be along the beam, it is not too difficult to stand with the other leg held out in front of you. But the moment you raise your heel the wobbles begin. Try

ABOVE: From the newest generation of Soviet artistry, the precocious Maria Filatova comes to wreck the idea that it takes experience to conquer the beam world

RIGHT: The German Democratic Republic have won a women's team medal in every world and Olympic tournament since 1968. Kerstin Gerschau was a Montreal winner

to turn even 90 degrees like that, and you are unlikely to survive; but the ball of the foot it must be, because the width of the beam does not allow for any greater contact than that. It begins to amaze you, does it not, that a gymnast can swiftly and securely pivot 360 degrees on that little beam four feet above the floor? They use a ballet trick to help them with that one: the eyes are fixed on a distant point straight ahead, and they hold it as long as possible while the body initiates the turn. As soon as the head must move, it is moved very quickly as far as possible, so that the eyes get back to the same point and hold it while the body catches up. But even that is not likely to save you on the sitting room carpet.

Dismounting

Whatever the standard of performance, there can be little doubt that the moment of dismount is the most critical of the exercise. The gymnast should aim not only for excellence in style and technique as she leaves the beam, but the highest standard of difficulty of which she is capable. Again, there are no restrictions on method. She may leave on her legs or her arms, from a static position or a fluid one, forwards, backwards or sideways, from the side of the beam or an end, and what she does on the flight off is up to her – as long as she lands on her feet and does not stagger.

The first few times out, the novice will be content, not to say relieved, just to jump off; but even that can be done in style. She will spring off the beam whichever way she chooses (and backwards is a bit tricky, because she cannot see where she is landing) with a good swing of the arms and an arched extension of the body in flight, as though she were coming off a vaulting horse. As she lands she will absorb the shock with slightly bent knees. When she is ready to make it harder, she may perform the same dismounts with a turn in the air, or with legs straddled.

As soon as handstands on the beam have been mastered, the gymnast can make a more spectacular exit. From the handstand she may push off with one arm, make a quarter or half turn and land beside the beam. She may cartwheel off, with or without a quarter turn in flight, and soon she will feel like tackling a handspring off the end of the beam, trying to keep her body straight in flight. One day, a lot later, the coach will encourage her to make a free dismount, by walkover or cartwheel (remembering to bring her legs together for landing), and if she ever becomes one of the angels it may be that she will perform a cartwheel to the end of the beam and spring off that into a twisting backward somersault. If, like most, she never gets quite that far, there will be nothing lost by thinking about it.

Queen of Munich and the world, Ludmilla Tourischeva.

13 Rings

Nikolai Andrianov of the USSR made history in 1976 when he became the first supreme Olympic champion to win a gold medal on the rings (a Yugoslav, Stukelj, won the combined exercises in the 1924 Games and the rings in 1928). Andrianov's quite extraordinary versatility – he also won the floor and the vault – deservedly make him an historic figure, but it does say something about the special problem the rings present that the achievement should have been unique. The isolation of this event goes further: in the history of the Olympic Games, only four times has the all-round champion figured even among the top three on the rings.

Their peculiar challenge is obvious: touch the rings and they move. To keep them under control while performing acrobatics on and around them requires a man of exceptional shoulder strength, and preferably one with short arms. No apparatus has provided more all-round champions than the pommel horse, and the pommels, which also demand substantial shoulder strength, favour the man with long arms.

The origins of the gymnastic rings lie in the circus trapeze bar. They were introduced early in the 19th century as a pair of short bars, and by the middle of that century had evolved into a pair of stirrup-like triangles on the end of short ropes (with knots in, for gripping), which themselves hung from what appeared to be a pair of rope ladders. The equipment was thus very adaptable, for the gymnast could swing or do 'muscle-up' stunts from the rungs of the ladders, the knots in the rope or the stirrups, and grip the rungs from the outside or the inside. By the beginning of the 20th century, the rings were more or less as we know them today, and as gymnastics began to interest the public, proved its most attractive feature. At about this time, the rings began to be used more and more for exhibitions of strength rather than swing, which was left to the high bar performers.

It was not until the Helsinki Games of 1952 that the gymnasts of the USSR (competing at the Olympics for the first time) showed the world with their voluntary exercises how much more there could be to a routine on the rings than power. Introducing the wheel to an astonished audience, they won the gold and silver rings medals at those and the next two Olympics (it took the Japanese that long to assemble what was to be their dominating challenge). Today, while it is true that no other gymnastic event gives such an opportunity for the exercise of strength, a performer cannot move into the top class without being able to swing fluently, and without conditioning his shoulder joints and muscles to an unnatural degree of flexibility.

The rings are now made of metal alloy and have an inside diameter of seven inches.

OVERLEAF LEFT: Regarded as the supreme test of strength on the rings, the technique of the crucifix eludes some good gymnasts. Shoulders and hands should be in line
OVERLEAF RIGHT: Almost the perfect straight body cross (crucifix) executed by Alexandr Detiatin (USSR), who was only beaten in Montreal by his compatriot Andrianov

The two Vladimirs, superb Soviet sports acrobats

Stan Wild (GB) should ideally have his arms closer to his sides in his 'L-support' at Munich. Men with short arms and strong shoulders are ideal for rings

They are attached by 2 ft 3 in (68.6 cm) straps to wire cables almost 18 inches (45.7 cm) apart. The cables are suspended from a framework 18 feet (5.48 m) high, but the rings hang at a maximum of less than 8 ft 3 in (2.51 m) from the ground – exactly the same height as the horizontal bar. You will usually see the coach steadying the rings before helping his man up to start the routine. In his optional exercises, the gymnast must include at least two movements of pure strength, and one of them must be a handstand. He must also perform another handstand through swing, rising from hang or support positions, and in general will aim to present a fluent succession of moves demonstrating fluidity, flexibility, strength in movement and static strength – holding, for instance, the famous 'cross'.

Some of the basic positions in which the gymnast swings, and from which he displays his strength, are the same as those he uses on the high bar – though this time, of course, additional physical qualities are needed. They are divided as usual into the positions of hang, in which the grip of the hands alone holds the gymnast, most of whose body is below the rings; and those of support, in which the strength of the arms holds up the gymnast, who may be totally above the rings (as in the handstand) or mostly below it (in bent arm support).

Front hang, in which the gymnast is at full stretch directly below the rings, is the least complicated position of all. He can move from there to bent hip hang by raising his hips, rounding his back and passing his legs between his arms, so that they are straight and horizontal, and he is folded in the tight pike position we have seen so often on other apparatus. The next position, the back hang, familiarly called 'skin the cat', will cause armchair gymnastic followers to wince: from the bent hip hang he rolls upright again, not by dropping his hips and letting his legs swing back the way they came, but by continuing the original movement. The hips roll higher still, the legs pass in front of his face towards the floor, and he hangs more or less vertically, though with his head and shoulders bending forward. It is as if you stood up in the sitting room and tried to touch the ceiling by raising your arms not in front, but behind you. It gives you some idea of the reason for that phrase 'an unnatural degree of flexibility'. Newcomers to the rings should not attempt the back hang until they have been expertly assisted to achieve that flexibility by proper exercises. Finally, the inverted hang, in which the gymnast is hanging upside down and vertically, with his arms by his sides and his hands gripping the rings by his thighs. That position can most easily be reached by raising the legs from a front hang and pulling hard on the rings. Advanced performers can do it without bending at the hips. Nobody should remain totally inverted like that for more than a few seconds.

A gymnast cannot begin to work in support positions without first developing the necessary shoulder strength. This is considerably more than he requires for identical positions on the parallel bars and the pommels, because of the unstable quality of the rings. In the standard front support position, he must control the rings so firmly

Just coming out of a dislocate, the disturbing move in which the gymnast appears to turn himself inside out and hang with his arms forced behind his back

that he can swing his legs forwards and backwards without making the rings swing. The arms should be held in line with the straps, with the upper body leaning only very slightly forward. Bent arm support is achieved by lowering the body from front support until the rings are at shoulder level, and L-support by raising the legs to the horizontal while the upper body and arms remain straight and between the cables.

From the 'L', the gymnast can rotate into a shoulderstand or a handstand, though the latter is not normally attempted by the novice. The performer leans forward and raises his hips (to retain a perfect sense of the centre of gravity is a vital matter in all movement on the rings). Simultaneously the arms, which were in straight support, are bent to lower the shoulders to ring level. When they are there, the legs are lifted between the cables to take the gymnast into a shoulder stand. The handstand needs the final crunch: a press up from there to straighten the arms and lock the elbows, with the rings pushed aside a little to make sure no part of the body touches the cable or its straps.

The young gymnast in his early days on the rings is always advised not to rush his progress. He should spend a long time moving from one static position to another, covering all those basic postures of hang and support over and over again, before venturing into anything more taxing. Incidentally, the expert coaches do not recommend weight-lifting and other strenuous muscle-building exercises as a preparation for work on the rings. They would rather see the novice devoting himself to exercises that will build his strength, and extend his suppleness, specifically in those areas where it will be needed. Anyway, as they are fond of telling you, strength alone will not enable you to become the lord of the rings.

Concurrent with his strength-building and basic positional exercises, the gymnast will be working to familiarize himself with the problems of controlled swing from two rings that are themselves only too ready to swing, independently not only of the gymnast but of each other. Little and often is the key to rings practice, because even hanging from the rings for more than a few seconds demands a strength that few of us have unless we work to acquire it. Hang swinging is the most natural activity to try first: it differs from hang swinging on the high bar in that the rings not only tend to

move backwards and forwards with the swing, but rise and fall as they do so. Accordingly, the body not only pivots on the rings through 180 degrees as it does on the bar, but if the gymnast cannot control the movement of the rings (as he must), it also describes a broader arc in the air.

On the forward part of the swing, the body starts (at the peak of a backswing) arched, passes through the vertical in the straight front hang position, and pikes slightly at the hips for the upward movement. At its conclusion, the arms bend as they pull the body up close to the rings for maximum height. On the way back, the gymnast should not 'work' at the swing, but let it fall naturally, body slightly arched as it passes the vertical, and legs leading the final stages of the backswing. At the peaks of each swing, the rings should be pushed more than shoulders' width apart. At an early stage, gymnasts are encouraged to practice simple dismounts from a hang swing. It does not take long for the performer to learn to swing powerfully forward, lift his legs and hips into an inverted hang and let the move flow on to a straight-body somersault dismount.

The swing in front support gives rise to balancing problems, and also presents the gymnast with the fact that the rings are going to move away from him as he pushes on them. He begins by strongly lifting his legs forward from the front support, allowing him a good downward and backward swing of the legs to set off the backward movement. At its peak, this should rise to well above the horizontal, but at all other times the gymnast has to keep his head and shoulders as close as possible to the vertical line.

It hardly needs pointing out that, before

Overall world champion in 1974, Shigeru Kasamatsu handstands on the rings in the Munich Olympics. The strap should be kept clear of the gymnast's arms

fully-controlled lowering of the body from shoulder stand to straight inverted hang. Again from front support, there is a useful move that takes him to a horizontal front hang with bent arms. This needs more than just a leaning back of the shoulders and swinging up of the legs: there must be a full-blooded forward swing in support, taking the legs above the horizontal; considerable strength is needed to control the fall back of the upper body.

Uprises

Probably the first manœuvre the gymnast learns after perfecting the hang swing is the front uprise. This begins in a forward swing and ends in L-support, or front support (for the advanced performer, it can end in a handstand). As usual in a forward swing, the body has been arched in its downward path, and the legs have swung forward after passing the vertical. The movement towards a pike is deliberately stopped before the gymnast reaches the horizontal, which sends the chest and hips up as the feet hang back. The gymnast then raises his wrists on the rings and spreads them wide, so that he ceases to pull them and instead pushes down on them, raising his shoulders between the cables. Though to go into front support requires further movement, as the legs swing down and back, it is of course much less of a strain for the novice, who may find holding the L-support too much for his abdominal muscles.

The back uprise follows a strong backward hang swing, and to set that in motion the gymnast usually starts in the inverted pike hang. He stretches his legs and hips vigorously upward, between the cables, so that his downswing comes all the way from

the gymnast moves on to the intriguing and impressive stunts with which he will want to make up his routine, he must spend many hours practising the links that take him from one position to another. Some are complicated enough to warrant careful examination, others are obvious enough for the beginner to work out his own path. Certainly he will soon need to find his way from front support to the piked hang (by leaning his shoulders back and moving his legs forward and up; or by rolling forward in a pike), and he will want to work on the care-

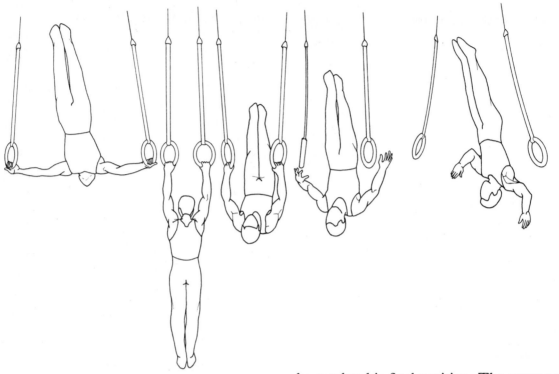

19 Rings: backwards full twisting dismount

the vertical. Power in the downswing is essential, for the legs must sweep through the lower vertical and rise behind the gymnast in a high, extended arch. It should be that movement, and not the strength of his arms, that carries his upper body up over the rings, with his arms remaining straight.

Kip

On the rings as anywhere else, the kip takes the gymnast from a hanging position directly to a support one on top of it, without the backward swing. It is a far more difficult move to perform on the rings than it is elsewhere, and the effort needed to achieve it often results in the beginner pitching forward and losing balance when

he reaches his final position. The gymnast needs to pass through a piked hang in which he rapidly closes his body to the tightest pike, and rapidly opens it again till his legs are about 45 degrees beyond the vertical. At the same time, using the powerful impetus this move has given him, he pushes hard down on the rings, bringing his upper body above them and letting his legs, which are straight throughout the move, swing down.

Dislocates

If you read the chapter on asymmetric bars, this term will be familiar to you. You will recall the dislocation catch, popular among advanced girl gymnasts, in which the arms are extended behind the back to catch the high bar. Earlier in this chapter, the backward hang ('skin the cat') arose, in which the gymnast was hanging with his arms behind his back. Both the forward and backward dislocation movements are used in the course of advanced tricks on the rings, and nobody can progress to the highest class without being able to master them. This involves not only patient physical preparation, but overcoming the natural mental reluctance to tackle an exercise with such an off-putting name. One can only reassure the newcomer to the rings that, as his own observation will prove, dislocates are eventually performed, and frequently, without the slightest inconvenience.

The forward-moving dislocation is performed at the horizontal peak of a hang backswing, and is known as inlocate. As the gymnast rises, face down, to the horizontal he pulls his arms towards his hips so that the rings move above, but outside, his shoulder blades. His arms are then rather in the position of wings on the upward beat.

At the same time the gymnast vigorously raises his hips, tucks his head down towards his chest and rolls into a piked hang.

In a dislocate, the body rolls backwards out of a piked hang towards a front hang swing, bringing the arms sideways and forwards as the body extends. The arms should be in the normal front swing position, with the rings held wide, by the time the body starts to swing forward. Experts achieve such perfection on the forward swing from a dislocate that they are able to conclude it with a handstand, reaching the position by swing alone, without ever bending their arms – a move known as a turn handstand. Dislocate dismounts, by the way, are taught as a step towards a full dislocate, apart from being useful in their own right. As he opens his body out of the pike and opens his arms out sideways, the gymnast releases the rings and goes into an arched body dismount.

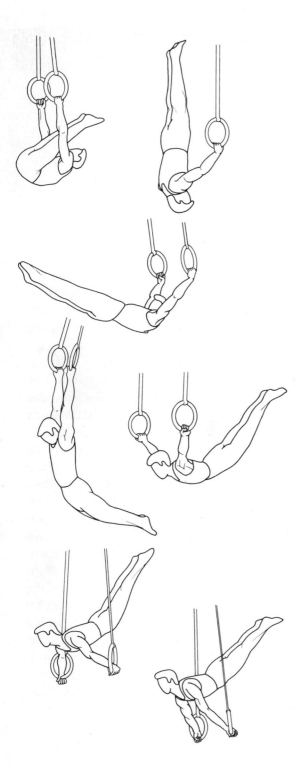

This, as a method of training, spares him the final swing forward of the arms.

Static strength

There is more to it than strength, of course, but there are several positions in which the exercise of unusual strength allied to technique and balance enable the gymnast to impress the judges. Most popular of all is the handstand, which has already been discussed, and the most dramatic is the straight body cross, a stunt that some gymnasts — even world-class ones — are never able to perform properly. Along the road towards those two, the worker on the rings will meet back and front levers, in both of which the body is held stretched and parallel to the ground. The back lever looks worse, but is the easier one in which to maintain balance. The body is face down and the rings should be approximately over the hips — the narrower the angle between the arms and the body the better. If the gymnast allows the angle to open up so that his body is lower and the rings are nearer his shoulders than his hips, he will find it impossible to keep his body straight and level. The easier grip for this move is the obvious one: the palms facing the rings, away from the body. Akitomo Kaneko is insistent that the advancing gymnast must learn the harder one, with the hands over the rings, palms facing down towards the body, because without it he will be greatly handicapped in moving from the back lever to support positions.

It is the fact that, in the back lever, the arms reach the limit of their movement in the shoulder sockets that makes the back lever easier to manage than the complemen-

20 Rings: backwards swing uprise

Okamura moved from straddle lever to planche, one of the most desperately difficult positions to hold properly. Shoulders must be well ahead of the rings

Japan's Teruichi Okamura getting everything just about as right as it could be in a straddle lever. Note the handgrips as well as the abundance of chalk

tary front lever. For that, the gymnast is again with a totally extended body and legs, his head held level and face up. Again, the rings should be above his hips, producing the narrow angle between arms and body. But this time the arms are not being forced against anything, and it takes tremendous muscle control in the shoulders to hold the position.

The planche presents a similar challenge. This is a position that advanced gymnasts demonstrate in their floor exercises, when they rise from the floor in full horizontal extension, face down, by hand pressure alongside the hips. It is an astonishing movement there, and must be perfected on the floor and on low parallel bars before it is attempted on the rings. When ideally executed, the body is absolutely straight from neck to toes, the head held up, no drooping in the midriff. To achieve that, the shoulders must be far forward of the rings,

and again this requires shoulder muscle power almost unbelievable to the spectator.

The stunt has not yet been devised in any phase of gymnastics that is more astounding than the straight body cross on the rings. To the uninitiated, the sight of a gymnast standing motionless on air, supported only by arms fully extended sideways at shoulder level, is as near a miracle as he is likely to see in sport. Is it done through superhuman strength alone? No, but it can hardly be done without it. Some exceptionally strong men find it impossible to master the technique, to channel their strength so precisely; conversely, the body cross has been perfectly executed by men of only average strength, because they have learned to use what they have with exquisite efficiency. Given the necessary power, the key to the perfect body cross lies in keeping the shoulders high and wide and the chest well out. Only with that basic framework will the arms be horizontal and the body vertical, and only then can this extraordinary pose be held for the requisite two seconds.

Dismounts

Despite their height, the instability of the

rings prevent the gymnast from executing as scintillating a dismount as he achieves from the high bar, but nevertheless the experts do bring off some marvellous twists and somersaults as they go. Before he aspires to such supremacy, the beginner will have polished his basic dismounts – from the forward swing, the backswing and the underswing (after a piked hang). He will have worked on the simple dislocate dismount mentioned earlier, and then he will move to his first somersault.

This is a progression from a strong forward hang swing. As he moves up from the vertical, the gymnast increases his speed with a sharp lift of his legs and a pull on the rings. The body should travel upward at least until the shoulders are level with the rings and the legs nearing the vertical, and at that moment he pushes down on the rings and releases them. This helps the body rotation to continue in the flight off, which he executes with a full stretched body and widespread arms. In an impressive extension of this dismount, the performer holds the rings longer, passing beyond the vertical, upside down, and straddles his legs wide outside the cables. He releases the rings as his legs swing down, completing the somersault in flight. A particularly strong arm pull is needed to accomplish this straddle back dismount.

Higher up the scale still comes a somersault dismount with full twist. This must be preceded by a very powerful forward swing, at the end of which the gymnast forces his body higher into the air by pushing down on the rings and thrusting his legs up. As he reaches the vertical, the hands leave the rings, pushing them wide, and the body stretches into its twist – a motion that is impelled by the transition from the bowed to the taut positions. As the legs fall through 180 degrees to complete the somersault, the trunk twists a full 360 degrees.

There is no way that a gymnast can be instructed on paper to perform such advanced feats. As for the double back somersault dismount, one can only describe it and prove that it actually happens. Another powerful forward hang swing is essential, at the peak of which the gymnast pushes down on the rings and lifts his knees towards his chest. As he tucks, he releases the rings, pushing them to the side again, and holds his knees in tight; this increases the speed of rotation. There must be body lift at the moment of release, or there will be no chance of having enough time and space to complete two somersaults and open the body out for landing. You have probably seen the greatest perform this marvellous movement, so you know it can be done: but even as it happens, spectators' lips are bitten in anxiety, for so often it looks as though he will not quite make it.

14 Competing, Scoring and Judging

It would be possible to make the scoring system in competitive gymnastics more complicated, but not much. It is certainly very doubtful whether the structure of the Olympic competition could possibly be more complex, or could produce so many gold medals in such a mystifying fashion. Of course everybody connected with the sport is delighted to see them, but there are times when one wonders how it all happened. Five days of competition in the modern pentathlon, for example, leads to two gold medals – one for the individual champion, one for the winning team. Four days of gymnastic endeavour brings 24 gold medals, 13 for men and 11 for women. Many followers of the sport fail to understand (and who can blame them?); how, for instance, Olga Korbut at Munich in 1972 could come top on the floor and the beam, second on the bars and fifth in the vault and yet be placed seventh in the overall combined exercises list. It seems sensible to try to explain here the way in which a major competition, such as the Olympics, or the world or European championships, is arranged, how it is scored, and what the judges are doing.

'Olympic gymnastics' does not necessarily refer to what happens at the Olympic Games. It is the term now used to denote the main stream of competitive gymnastics across the world, separating that primarily from educational gymnastics, recreational gymnastics, and such competitive branches of the parent body as modern rhythmic gymnastics, sports acrobatics, tumbling and trampolining. Olympic gymnastics comprises exercises on six different pieces of equipment (including the floor mat) for men, and four for women. The Olympics always open with the team competitions, in which every contesting nation must enter six gymnasts (of each sex, if both men's and women's titles are being contested).

It often happens in the Olympic Games that some of the weaker gymnastic nations do not have, or are not able to enter, as many as six gymnasts of the required standard. They nevertheless have to take part in the team competition, for reasons that will shortly be obvious, and are usually put together in convenient groups. In Montreal, for instance, the three British girls performed the team exercises with the two Belgian girls; the three British men were with two Australians. Obviously, the combined scores of such a group are not totalled. They are all competing only as individuals.

Men compete with exercises on the floor (in fact, a mat from which the gymnast is able to extract a little bounce), the pommel horse (sometimes called the side horse), the vaulting horse (or long horse), the rings, the parallel bars and the high bar (horizontal bar). Women meet on the floor, vaulting horse (sideways for them), balance beam and asymmetric bars (high and low bars). Statistical details of all these pieces of apparatus appear in the chapters of this book devoted to them individually. Except in the individual apparatus final there is no regulation order in which they must be tackled. For the sake of organizational efficiency, it is customary, where possible, to hold major competitions in an arena big enough to take all the apparatus at once, with the necessary surrounding areas, and to divide the competitors into equal-sized groups. Each begins the competition on a different piece of apparatus, and moves to the next when every group is ready.

The organizers of all major competitions have to devise, for each piece of apparatus, a compulsory exercise to be performed by every gymnast. The precise details of all compulsories are circulated to competing nations long in advance of the event, so that the gymnasts have ample time to master the required skills and polish the routine. In the case of the vault, the compulsory requirements are simple enough, but for the women's floor exercise in the Montreal Olympics there were some 80 instructions to be memorised. A segment from them: 'Step forward on right foot and turn three-eights to right on right foot; step forward quickly and take hurdle step into dive cartwheel with quarter turn back; take two mounter flip-flaps into lunge ...'

In the Olympic Games, the first day of the gymnastic competition is devoted to the compulsory exercises (male and female at different times) and the second day to the gymnasts returning to the scene and performing a voluntary, or optional, exercise on each piece of equipment. This is when the flair and brilliance of the performer is seen to its best, and it is not uncommon for the best gymnasts to score more highly on the optional and the weaker ones more highly on the compulsories. At the end of that, every competitor has two sets of marks. For the purpose of calculating the team scores, the lowest individual score in each exercise is ignored. This sensible arrangement ensures that a team's chances are not wrecked if one member is injured during an exercise and has to withdraw. Each team's best five compulsory scores and best five optional scores are totalled to determine the final placings in the team competition. So far, so good.

Now: every individual competitor's two scores are also totalled, and the top 36 (of each sex) go on to contest the all-round titles, or what are officially called the combined exercises individual championships. In the 1976 Olympic Games a condition was added at this stage: that of the final 36, not more than three competitors may be from any one nation. For this final, decisive round each gymnast must perform once more on each piece of apparatus an optional exercise that may, or may not, be the same one performed during the team competition. The marks for this final round are added not to the total score obtained by the individual during the team competition, but to half that total – or the average of his compulsory and optional scores. The winner of that is the all-round Olympic champion, the greatest gymnast of the day. You will see that, because of the large number of component parts that make up the individual's final total score (18, in the case of men), consistent all-round ability will win the day. Under pressure from the steady performer who ranks second or third in every exercise, the most brilliant gymnast is not likely to win the all-round gold medal if he has one weakness, or suffers just one disaster.

So that has looked after the team championships and the combined individual championships. The concluding stages are devoted to the individual apparatus championships. Only six gymnasts contest each one – the six with the highest scores on each apparatus at the end of the team competition. Their scores in the final round of the combined individual championships are not counted. Again, at each apparatus final, the gymnast starts with half the total of the marks he obtained in the team competition, those first two rounds. He then performs one more optional exercise on the apparatus, the marks for which are added to his preliminary score to decide the winner.

It can now be made clear, or at least clearer, what happened to Olga Korbut in 1972. She performed excellently throughout the team competition and entered the final round of the combined individual contest in third place, with a preliminary total of 38.35 out of a possible 40. In three of the four elements of the final round she continued to perform excellently, and was likely to have won the all-round silver medal but for a disaster on the asymmetric bars. She received only 7.50 marks and dropped to seventh place all-round. Then Korbut came to the individual apparatus finals. Because of her consistently high marks during the team competition she was contesting all of them, and was not handicapped by that disastrously low score because it happened during the all-round final. She went on, as you read earlier, to complete the Games with two golds and a silver.

If the structure of a major competition is now clear, you may take the ice pack off your head and we will look more closely at the qualities a gymnast is expected to display on each apparatus, and get an idea of the way the judges apportion the marks. At any major international meeting, the corps of judges is usually composed of one judge from each of the competing nations. Four judges and one superior judge preside at

each apparatus, helped where necessary by line judges, time judges and those whose job is not to award marks, but to check that the compulsory exercises are being performed accurately. The superior judge is responsible for the work and decisions of the others, and (as you may occasionally have seen) will call them into a huddle if he thinks one of them has marked unfairly. In effect, one unduly biased mark, for better or for worse, does not affect the competitor's score: of the four judges' marks, the highest and the lowest are discounted and the gymnast is awarded the average of the remaining two.

However, there is a further safeguard. If there is an unusual discrepancy between the two middle marks, and if these two judges refuse to alter them, the 'base mark' is used. For this, the mark awarded (but not otherwise used) by the superior judge is needed. It is added to the average of the two middle marks, and the resulting total divided by two to produce a new average.

Every exercise is marked out of a possible ten points. In World and Olympic set exercises, there is no statutory breakdown of that maximum, but in all optional exercises, five points are for execution and five for composition.

The marks in the optionals are greatly influenced by the standard of difficulty of the exercise, which on its own can win three of the five composition marks. Within the detailed maxima for amplitude, execution and so on, the judges have explicit instructions, laid down in the International Code of Points, as to what deductions are to be made for what offences. They range from a loss of 0.10 for incorrect positioning of toes to 0.50 or more being deducted for serious loss of amplitude throughout the exercise, or bending of the body or limbs when not permitted.

Vaulting, the briefest and most explosive of all exercises, is a case on its own. Each vault in the optionals must be declared in detail to the judges beforehand, who then award it the tariff of difficulty laid down in the Code of Points. Every competitor may perform two vaults in both the compulsory and the optional exercises, and the higher score awarded is the one recorded. The two optional vaults may differ, and for every two vaults, the gymnast may take one extra trial run, as long as he does not touch the horse. On landing, the male gymnast (but not the female) may take one step without penalty, providing it is in the direction of the descent and is not caused by loss of balance.

Judges of the men's floor exercises are looking for flexibility, balance, hold and strength; and for creativity and imagination. Over-long runs and lack of height in jumps and somersaults are among the many defects that will be punished. The women are examined for sureness and acrobatics, turns and balances; for general posture; for coordination, lightness, suppleness and relaxation. A woman's optional sequences must be varied and original, suit her build and temperament, and be put together in such a way that she can display both artistry and gymnastic ability. It is important that men's and women's exercises form a logical and harmonious whole, are smoothly assembled, and use the whole floor space without the competitor putting a foot outside it.

Though the parallel bars exercise demands, and must be seen to be given, a measure of strength, the judges want movements of swing and flight to dominate. In the individual events, a gymnast must in-

clude certain moves of special difficulty, in which both from above the bars and under them, he releases his grip with both hands at the same time and regrasps in the same way. During the team competition, this need only be done once, from either above or below. The competitor will be penalized if in any one performance, he remains motionless more than three times.

On the high bar, the gymnast who wants to record a maximum score has to include one combination in which, as on the parallels, he lets go of, and regrasps, the bar with both hands at once. There must be absolutely no stops on this apparatus, and the judges carefully watch to see that the optional exercise includes changes of grip, twists and as many variations of circle as possible, including both forward and backward giant swings.

On the asymmetric bars, the female gymnast is judged chiefly on her swinging movements, on the passage of her body between bars, on changing hand grips on each bar and – in her optional – on the difficulty of the elements she introduces. Only two gymnasts from any one team can use identical mounts or dismounts, and nobody may dismount by a somersault from the low bar. Should she have the misfortune to fall, she will certainly be heavily penalized; but as long as she resumes within 30 seconds, the exercise may go on.

Falls from the balance beam must be corrected within ten seconds, and in her optional exercise the gymnast must be careful to make use of the whole length of the beam and to vary the tempo throughout. Again, it must be a continuous exercise, with three brief pauses allowed to demonstrate balance. Judges do not like to see too many sitting or lying positions in a beam

The graceful Elvira Saadi in full flight for the broad horse

routine, which must contain one full spin and one leap.

The pommel horse is for swinging on, but more often than not it is lack of strength that causes the gymnast to come to grief. He must never grind to a halt, or let his legs more than lightly brush the horse. For high scoring in the optional, he must 'travel' all over the horse, spend most of his time doing double-leg circles, and be sure to include both forward and reverse scissors – at least one of which must be executed twice in succession.

On the rings (the stationary rings, as they are hopefully called in official language), the gymnast's greatest problem is to persuade the judges that he did not unnecessarily move them. He must swing (but they must not), he must demonstrate strength – including 'hold' elements. At least two hand-stands must be in the optional routine.

It is not likely that any major competition is completed without some public – and a lot of private – dissension over the judging. It is just the same in ice skating and any other sport in which personal opinion is influential in determining a competitor's score, and there are some who believe that, for that reason alone, such activities do not belong in competitive sport at all. All one can be sure is that in gymnastics everything possible has been done to narrow the judges' options, to force them to conform to rules and behave more like recording machines than human beings. If there are times when emotion, even passion, overtake mechanical precision – well, gymnastics on the whole is none the worse for that.

Among the greatest non-Soviets, Karin Janz (GDR)

15 Sports Acrobatics

The Greeks had a word for everything. *Gymnos* was theirs, and so was *akrobatos* – it meant to climb aloft, to raise oneself to the heights, to walk on tiptoe. There was probably never a time when the world was without some sort of acrobats. We know that, long before the Greeks, the ancient Egyptians were familiar with somersaults and handstands and backflips, because little sculptures showing them have been found in tombs. There is even some pictorial evidence in Sweden of similar activities taking place 4,000 years ago, in the time of neolithic man.

William the Conqueror brought tumblers over from Europe to Britain in 1066, and through the Middle Ages there were wandering troupes of tumblers in Europe, Asia and Africa. In the time of the cultural renaissance of the 15th and 16th centuries there was in Venice an annual 'concourse of living architecture', at which human pyramids more than 30 feet (9.14 m) high were seen, and in 1599 the sport's first handbook appeared: 'Three dialogues on the exercise of jumping and performing acrobatics in the air,' by Archiange Tuccaro.

In time, acrobatics came to include tumblers, equilibrists - (balancers), contortionists, tightrope walkers and trapeze artists. Some form of tightrope activity had been known in ancient Greece, but the trapeze was invented in 1859 by the French acrobat named Leotard – the same year that his compatriot Blondin (real name Jean-Francois Gravelet) first walked on a tightrope 160 feet above Niagara Falls. Trapeze

work was mostly seen in circuses, which began early in the 19th century to add variety to what had earlier been primarily a display of horsemanship (Philip Astley, a former army sergeant-major, formed the first 'modern' circus in 1768).

By the end of the 19th century acrobats of all kinds were a major attraction of circus life. Tumbling had not at that time developed within the framework of modern gymnastics. It fitted neither the 'strength on apparatus' philosophy of Jahn, nor Ling's 'free expression in physical training' conception. As the floor exercises gained greater freedom through the early 20th century, aspects of tumbling began to be included; but those gymnasts who found the greatest appeal in the more acrobatic elements of tumbling stayed with it and tumbling was included as a separate event in the Olympic Games of 1932, in Los Angeles (but never again). Many adherents took up trampolining during or after the Second World War (for some years that sport was known as rebound tumbling), and in 1965 the first world tumbling championships were held at the Albert Hall, London, in conjunction with the second world trampoline championships. That partnership persisted, with the world tumbling championships being held every other year from 1969.

Meanwhile, a new and exciting arm of gymnastics was beginning to flex. Acrobatics had for long been particularly popular in the Soviet Union, where they were accepted as a separate sport, and from there Bulgaria and Poland became deeply in-

Sports acrobatics provides some of gymnastics' most thrilling and entertaining moments. Competitors must show strength and balance as well as agility

Women work in singles, pairs and threes, and like these Soviet performers need a strong anchor at the base and a lighter, more agile balancer at the top

volved. For more than 20 years these three nations have led the world in sports acrobatics, which now has a real life of its own. A congress was held in Moscow in November 1973, and the International Federation of Sports Acrobatics was formed. The world championships were held in Moscow in 1974, in Saarbrucken, West Germany, in 1976 and in Varna, Bulgaria in 1978. Eight nations and 88 acrobats contested the first, ten nations and 150 acrobats the second. In the alternate years, World Cup competitions were held – in Switzerland in 1975 and Poland in 1977.

Apart from the three Eastern Bloc nations, Britain is the world's most experienced competitor, and enjoys some individual successes in the open tournaments staged by the big three.

The sport is growing very fast in the United States, which has its own magazine, *AcroSports*, and an outstanding competitor in Steve Elliott, who in the 1977 World Cup won three silver medals and produced a triple-twisting, double back somersault. In the USSR, however, there is even a woman who regularly performs a double layout somersault, an achievement that would have been thought physically impossible ten years ago.

Solo tumbling (officially known as acrobatic jumps) is not the beginning and the end of sports acrobatics, but it is its most vigorous element and the one that demonstrates the greatest agility, and so is the most immediately popular. Each competitor performs two sequences, known as runs or passes, on a strip 25 metres long (about 27 yards) and 1½ metres wide (five feet). He (or she) is allowed a run-up of no more than 10 metres, and may take off from a springboard of the Reuther type. In competition, the strip is now usually a felt-covered sprung sandwich of plywood and foam rubber, or (ideally) what is called a ski run. This is a runway which, when it was first devised, was almost unbelievably made of 600 cross-country skis covered first with a foam mat and then a felt pad. It helps the performer achieve tremendous elevation, but is not the sort of apparatus for which many gyms can find room.

It is not unusual for competitors from the newer and weaker nations in this sport to arrive for world championships and meet the 'ski run' for the first time. One such, in a warm-up at the second world championships on the new tumbling platform, reached such unaccustomed height on a layout back somersault that he was nowhere near the floor when he thought he was, landed on his back and rebounded eighteen inches (half-a-metre).

The competitor's first run must include three types of somersault, but no twist of more than 180 degrees. To rate the full ten-point difficulty tariff, men must include a triple somersault and women a double. The second run has to include twists of 180 degrees or more, and in both of them the competitor must maintain or increase his initial speed.

The routines devised by the greatest tumblers are beyond the imagination of those of us whose experience is limited to watching the standard gymnastic floor exercises on a mat. The first pass of the USSR winner of the 1976 world championships, Yuri Zikunov, comprised a round-off, flic-flac, a double layout back somersault, two flic-flacs and a double tucked back somersault. Britain's leading competitor, Morgan Smith, wrote of him in *AcroSports*: 'The way this man moves down the tumbling runway can be likened to the take-off of Concorde.' The runner-up, also of the USSR, was a schoolboy, Vladim Bindler. Wrote Morgan Smith: 'Every time I see this boy prepare his express timed run I literally stop breathing. He propels himself forward five to ten feet into the round-off which in turn produces the most efficient flic-flac in the world; then blasts himself skywards rotating at a ridiculous speed to land after turning three somersaults.' It was at the same championships that the young Russian female student, Ludmilla Zyganova, produced her double back layout somersault after a round-off and a flic-flac.

The five other events of sports acrobatics are all deeply dependent on team work, a rare occurrence in gymnastics. There are classes for men's and women's pairs, mixed pairs, women's trios and a men's group of four. In each event, including the tumbling, the gymnasts have to perform two compulsory and two voluntary exercises. In all the team work, the first exercise is designed to show balance and strength, and the second is judged on tempo – movement and flight. They are all performed on a regular gymnastic mat (12 metres square) and have

Mixed pairs work often produces incredible feats like this, but the crowd's favourite is usually the pyramid built four men high on one pair of feet

less weight and advanced powers of balance. All the routines are performed to music except the first exercises in men's pairs and fours. When you consider the men's fours, the physical achievement is often spectacular. The first exercise consists of a set pyramid (i.e., tower of bodies), or a transition (changing) pyramid, or two different set pyramids. The USSR fours winners at the Saarbrucken world championships built a pyramid of three men upright (two standing on the shoulders below them), with the fourth man doing a one-armed handstand, unsupported, on the head of the third. The four seconds for which it is necessary to hold these pyramids must sometimes seem like an eternity.

The 'tempo' exercise consists mainly of throws and somersaults in the circus tradition. In Saarbrucken the Poles, for example, featured a one-and-a-half layout back somersault executed by a man who was doing a handstand on the head of a man who was standing on the shoulders of another. He was caught by the fourth man, thus giving rise to the description, in their peculiar jargon: 'a layout back $1\frac{1}{2}$ from a 3-high handstand to a catch.'

Women's trios attach some importance, as you might expect, to the choreography of both exercises, and individual as well as group work is judged. They too build pyramids of considerable complexity, though the overall height of their human towers seldom equals the combined height of the group. They are more likely to stand on the thighs of the bottom gymnast than her shoulders, but the generally greater flexibility of women gymnasts does enable them to build more beautiful and varied pyramids than the men do. They too must hold their set pyramid for four seconds, but in the

differing time limits. In adult competition, competitors must be at least 14 years old and there must not be more than ten years difference in the ages of partners.

Despite the variety and agility that is included in the team work, it is all based on one person of great strength and stability supporting another (or several others) of

words of the International Federation rules, 'the music and movement must be choreographed to make a feminine feeling.' Three minutes is allowed for each exercise, which overall should be a work of art.

Pairs work often produces the most fascinating gymnastics of the lot, with the women in particular getting the chance to demonstrate not only agility, balance and choreography, but individual acrobatic elements in unison. Mixed pairs sees the finest combinations of strength and balance, with the favourite ploy of a man holding aloft at full stretch, with one hand grasping one foot, a girl in an arabesque. Even the women's pairs, at the highest class, seem to have no trouble in hand-to-hand balances and in their tempo exercises, spring lightly from the floor to a position of support over their partner's head, or whirl prettily together through a synchronized handspring in which they hold each other's inside hands and spring off the outside hand only.

In 1975 the West Germans introduced a new sports acrobatics creation to the world: pedestal balancing. In this, the gymnast performs hand balancing feats on a low pedestal with a rectangular top, approximately six inches by seven inches. Though quite often seen in exhibition work, the pedestal has not been approved for international competition. Most nations feel that the introduction of apparatus into sports acrobatics would deprive it of one of its most appealing features – the absolute simplicity of the operation. Though in international competition it is splendid to be able to perform the acrobatic jumps from a ski run, there is no need for the club gymnast to be provided with anything other than a Reuther board and mats for the entire sport

to be open to him. This fact alone should make it immensely attractive and useful to schools, and no doubt those nations who can develop the sport at the roots will be the ones who in the end give the strongest competition to the East European leaders.

Certainly the sport is spreading, Hungary, West Germany, Britain and America are ahead of the second class field at the moment, but they may have to work hard to hold their places. In Europe, France, Switzerland and Portugal have now taken it up; Cuba, Egypt and Mexico have entered the field. So have Japan, and who would like to predict how far they will rise? And what of China? Though they are still outside the international federation, their sports acrobatics were sufficiently advanced for them to give an enthralling display in London in the summer of 1977. It was not up to the breathtaking standard of the Soviet experts (as usual with the Chinese, there was no attempt to develop personality), but there were girl tumblers doing two-and-a-half twist somersaults, and the men's pair emulated the Soviets in the astonishing single-hand handstand on the head of the partner in full planche on the floor.

In many of the slowly-emerging gymnastic nations, sports acrobatics is still a meaningless phrase. Even in Britain, where gymnastics altogether has risen both through participant strength and spectator appeal to the status at least of a major minor sport, there are few people outside the 500 or 600 practitioners who have ever heard of sports acrobatics. It is difficult to doubt, however, that with an enthusiastically-administered development plan and more international competition, this branch of the sport has an exciting future in Britain and the world.

16 Modern Rhythmic Gymnastics

Ever since Ling's rhythmic Swedish gymnastics took root in Europe in the mid-19th century, there has been a quiet, but gradually blooming, branch of the sport that embraces the concept of gymnastic movement without violent action or muscular stress, or the use of any fixed apparatus. Though what we now know as Olympic gymnastics grew away from Ling and settled much closer to Jahn, there have always been those who desired no more than the rhythmic execution of free-flowing exercises, in which the essential qualities needed are those of suppleness, grace, balance, coordination and – to some degree – balletic art.

It is a century since rhythmic gymnastics were introduced to Britain, and they came to the United States in 1889. In both countries, the activity became known as recreative gymnastics, but it was on the continent of Europe, and notably in France, that it gained the greatest favour. There *gymnastique moderne* was its name, and today the English-speaking world knows it as modern rhythmic gymnastics. Meanwhile, the idea had encouraged many enthusiasts, of whom between the two World Wars the members of the Women's League of Health and Beauty became internationally famous for their mass demonstrations of rhythmic exercises.

Modern rhythmic gymnastics, however, has long since ceased to be merely a 'keep fit' recreation. It is far more demanding than that, requiring of its adherents skill, determination and long hours of training. It is also a competitive sport, and one serious enough to have had its own world championships every other year since 1963. It is administered internationally by a special section of the world ruling body, the Fédération Internationale de Gymnastique, which has laid down the extremely precise requirements of the sport in competition.

It is performed only by women, and always with music, and in that respect the relation between the sight and the sound must be even closer than it is in the women's floor exercises in Olympic gymnastics. The composition of the exercise has to correspond in rhythm and character to the musical accompaniment, and the choreography must be in close harmony with the music. The music must be expressive, rhythmic and at times lively, and should appear to be inseparable from the movement. As in the Olympic floor work, it may only be played by a single instrument and a single musician. The area on which the exercises are performed is also the same as for Olympic work – twelve metres square, and as much of the area as possible should be used. It may be covered with a mat or carpet, or it may not, but in top-class competition two areas of that size are provided, one of which is covered, and the gymnast can use either.

The most appealing aspect of modern rhythmic gymnastics is its beautiful use of ribbons and balls, but soloists must also work without them. The exercise without hand apparatus must last between 90 seconds and two minutes, and differs considerably from the Olympic floor exercise. Agility is not a requirement, and no form

Modern rhythmic gymnastics combines the agility and grace of the sport with elements of dance and the dexterity of a juggler. It is essentially feminine

Hoops, balls, ropes and clubs are used, solo and by teams, but the most fascinating displays are often with the ribbon – six metres (19 ft) of satin on a stick

of acrobatic tumbling is allowed. It is a dance routine that demonstrates the flexibility and perfect coordination of the gymnast, and contains a great variety of steps, leaps, turns, pivots, hops and balances, with every element fitting the music.

Spinal suppleness of a kind only enjoyed by a gymnast is an absolute necessity before perfection can be approached. The spine of the accomplished rhythmic gymnast bends in all directions, far enough for her to be able to touch the floor behind her, and to enable the trunk to describe a circle around her. Such movements of the spine are known as flexions, and these may be used with the limbs and the head and neck to produce waves, as the body ripples sinuously from one extreme to the other. Like an

Olympic gymnast, she will include in her performance occasional held scales, or balances, in which she briefly freezes her routine in a pose that should show beauty as well as balance accomplishment. Turns are as difficult to execute satisfactorily as they are on the beam, because they must be made only on the toes of one foot. Jumps should be high, long, light and lively.

Apparatus exercises are immensely effective and often extraordinarily skilful. There are five standard pieces of equipment accepted in competition, and each one has to be so used that it becomes an extension of the body. It must be constantly moving, never at rest, and for each one there are certain detailed skills that have to be mastered if the competitor is to gain high marks from

One of the world's greats, Natalia
Krascheninnikova of the Soviet Union. As usual,
it is the Eastern Europeans who have led the sport
from the start

the judges. All solo apparatus exercises
must last between 60 and 90 seconds.

The rope, the length of which is determined by the height of the gymnast, can be
used for skipping, and for expert extensions
and variations on the basic skipping movements; but it is also extensively used as an
item of counter-balancing and harmonic
accompaniment to the gymnast's dancing
and balancing movements. It can be swung,
thrown and cast around the body, by one
end or by two. It must always be in motion
and must always appear in an unbroken
line.

Gold, silver and bronze are colours that
are forbidden for any apparatus. The hoop
can be any other colour, or of unpainted
wood, and in senior competition should

have an internal diameter of between 0.80
and 0.90 metres. Its use and movement fall
into six categories. It may be held at arm's
length and swung from the shoulder around
and about the body – swinging, balancing
and circumduction. It can be turned or
twisted, by one hand or two – turning. It
can be made, and very often is, to rotate
around any part of the body, and most commonly between the thumb and first finger
– rotation. It can be thrown and caught, but
the catching must be neither jerky nor
static; the movement must always be flowing, involving the whole body – throwing
and regrasping. It may be rolled, either on
the floor or across some part of the gymnast
– rolling; and while it is so moving, the
gymnast can jump over it or find some way
of passing through it, or she can pass the
hoop over her body while she is jumping in
the air – passing over and through.

Using the ball presents a special challenge, because it must never be held, even
when being caught. It can be of rubber or
plastic, must weigh at least 400 grams
(about 14 ounces), and have a diameter of
between 18 and 20 centimetres (7–8 inches).
The performer can roll it on the floor or
across her body, which produces some
delicately attractive sights as it travels, for
instance, along one arm, across the chest and
down the other arm; and she can spin it
between her hands – rolling and rotation.
She can bounce it, but not with the flat
patting movement that is natural to most of
us; it must be a supple movement in which
the whole body takes part and the hand and
wrist remain flexible – bouncing. Without
ever gripping, and always allowing it to roll
freely in and out of the hand, it may be
thrown and caught – throwing and catching. Again without ever holding it in the

fingers, the ball may be balanced in the palm of the hand while the arm swings and circles in the air – balancing/swinging.

The most beautiful and intriguing section of the whole sport, and many think of the whole movement of gymnastics, is the exercise with the ribbon, that produces such marvellous twirling patterns. The ribbon is six metres (6½ yards) long, between four and six centimetres (1½–2⅓ inches) wide, and is attached to a slender, wand-like stick between 50 and 60 centimetres long (nearly two feet). It should be of satin or some similar material, and the method by which it is attached to the stick must allow the maximum freedom of movement to the ribbon.

There are five classifications of ribbon movement. Swings and circles are performed from the shoulder, with the arm straight (but moving, at will, in different planes and different directions), and produce large arcs of ribbon, which must remain in an unbroken curve. Snaking, either up and down or sideways, makes waves in the ribbon that must run down its entire length. Spirals are made by a 'stirring' action of the wrist and forearm, and the ribbon takes on a series of concentric circles from end to end, that can be of the same size or of gradually increasing size. Figure of eight is a more complex but most impressive manoeuvre, particularly when the size of the figure and the speed with which it is drawn is varied. Finally, the very difficult operation of throws, which are only attempted by the most expert – throwing a stick up and catching it may be easy, but six metres of ribbon on the end of it is another matter.

Clubs (two are always used) with long, slender necks and bulbous bodies are particularly attractive when used in group work. They are between 40 and 50 centimetres (15¾–19⅔ inches) long and each weigh 150 grams (about 5¼ ounces), and usually have a small ball-shaped head by which they are lightly held between the fingers. With straight arms, they may be swung and circled from the shoulder as an extension of the arms. The movement of the two clubs need not necessarily be either simultaneous or identical – swings and circles. They can be twirled by the wrist alone – twirls; thrown, one at a time or both together, and caught either by the head or the body – throws; or rhythmically beaten together, or on the floor beats, which adds the dimension of sound to the performance.

Though there is probably no more impressive sight in modern rhythmic gymnastics than ribbon work, there is no doubt that the clubs provide the greatest test of skill, dexterity and coordination.

Imagine, if you have never had the chance to see it, those exercises performed by a team of six gymnasts for between two-and-a-half and three minutes, and you begin to sense the full beauty and excitement of which this branch of the sport is capable.

Each member may use one or two pieces of the same equipment, and at least four times during the exercise the apparatus must be exchanged between members of the team – and each time in a different way. At the same time, the team must be making at least six different formations on the floor. The judges will be marking not only the technical efficiency of each individual and of their group work, but also the quality of the whole choreography, its originality, and the harmony, precision and amplitude of its execution.

17 Gymnastics at School

It is more true of gymnastics than of any other Olympic sport, that it is shaped, and its progress determined, by the quality and enthusiasm of its teaching in schools. Those nations whose international achievements remain lamentably low are almost certain to be those in which gymnastics have pathetically low priority in the educational curriculum, and probably exist at all only as a recreational activity ('Come on everyone, now let's be sunflowers') rather than as a competitive one.

You can be sure that this is no problem in Eastern Europe, but in the West, and specifically in Britain, youngsters tend to develop into major gymnasts not because of, but despite, the way they have been taught at school. For most of us who were in our childhood before or during the Second World War, gymnastic activity consisted mainly of a daily session of 'PT' – perhaps 15 minutes of formal, static, group exercises in arm swinging and stretching combined with knees bending, astride jumping and the occasional handstand. Apparatus in primary schools was unheard of and in secondary schools was, more often than not, disused. More adventurous gymnastic activities had fallen strongly out of favour, perhaps because of a fear among the authorities that they were dangerous. Even within the better-equipped English public school system, 'gym' only meant an hour a week with wall bars, ropes, mats and the vaulting horse and failure to conform to average achievements was often met by scathing criticism, or physical punishment.

The return of teachers from service in the armed forces, where training on 'assault courses' had become standard practice, led to a generally less constricted approach. There was, wrote the authors of *Activities on P.E. Apparatus* (J. Edmundson and J. Garstang, 1962), a growing awareness that children naturally wanted to run and climb and jump, and that activities they actually enjoyed might fit into the PE curriculum despite the prejudice against them. Those dreary, formalized arm and leg movements gradually gave way to freer, more graceful exercises (back to Ling again), and apparatus was brought back to the gyms that twenty years earlier had been thrown out. Of greatest importance, the recent experiences of the teachers had banished their fear for the safety of the child, which naturally had been conveyed to the pupils.

Edmundson and Garstang conceded that as the child grows older, his interest in apparatus work decreases, and that very few adults ever enter a gymnasium. So was it not a waste of time and money to introduce apparatus into the school programme at all? A fallacious argument, they contend: 'At some period in the development of the individual there is an innate desire for the physical expression that apparatus allows. It plays an important part in the physical development of the human body.'

At about this time a Government publication noted that in nursery school physical activity there was no element of competition and no urging the child to do something more difficult than he chose himself:

'It appears that older children are also perfectly capable of assessing their powers, and that they do not attempt the feats of the very few agile children, provided they are not urged to reach a common level of achievement. When faced with a new movement, or unknown piece of apparatus, most children usually show caution and explore the situation carefully until they have thoroughly tested their powers. This caution, and the tendency to careful exploration, are evident in all children in the primary range.' (HMSO: 'Planning the Programme: P.E. in the primary school').

Desirable though it was to remove from young children the harsher elements of competition in the gym, that inevitably led to an educational attitude that has had the most unfortunate effect on Olympic (i.e. competitive) gymnastics. At the time Edmundson and Garstang produced their book, a few enthusiasts in the Midlands of England were forming the English Schools Gymnastic Association, primarily to foster and encourage competitive gymnastics in schools, and to provide an outlet for those frustrated pupils whose gymnastic ability was not severely tested by a life as snowflakes and sunflowers.

The EGSA had become a strong influence in the sport, with an annual income that has risen from the initial £40 to £12,000. They compete frequently in Europe, and in 1976 won the World Schools Games (in which some of the most powerful nations did not compete). But their efforts to persuade schools, and more particularly the local authorities that control them, to use Olympic apparatus in their gyms, have two massive obstacles to clear – one understandable and the other not.

The financial restrictions in education have added to the attractions of purely recreational gymnastics, or to the maintenance of no more than the apparatus already installed. A PE programme with no more ambitious involvement than that is relatively cheap and easy to run, and does not require – and here comes the second hurdle – specialized gymnastic coaching. A PE teacher has to be jack of all sports, and is most unlikely to be master of gymnastics unless he is one of the rare creatures who practised the sport competitively. The training colleges, the physical education training colleges, are still seldom turning out qualified gymnastic coaches, so what chance do the children have?

If they are lucky, they may find a teacher who is at least sympathetic and who can encourage the keen and talented ones to join a local club where facilities do exist. Alas, there are still by no means enough of these to satisfy the huge demand created by Korbut and the 1972 Olympics, and most of those that exist are under-equipped and under-coached. Indeed, it is to the educational authorities that the sport should be able to turn for help. It is the school gymnasia, fully equipped with normal competitive apparatus, that should, after school hours, be the home of all the local voluntary gymnasts. In Britain, the boot is on the other foot and it does not even fit. No amount of eager patching and squeezing is going to overcome the basic need for the shoemaker and his patrons to get their priorities right. Until they do, neither Britain, nor any other nation that operates in a similar fashion, can hope to challenge the world's gymnastic leaders.

18 Trampolining

Gymnastics' greatest joy comes in about 96 square feet (8.9 sq.m) of woven webbing stretched within a metal frame. No instrument devised by man for physical exercise is more certain to banish gloom and sweeten sour tempers. Just try being unhappy on a trampoline – third bounce and the smiles break through.

Over the past 20 years, trampolining has made steady progress as a sport and spectacular progress as a recreational activity. Without great physical effort or complex involvement, it is immensely enjoyed from nursery school to senility. Simple bouncing calls for some discipline, but scant training, and the four basic 'drops' are soon mastered. With no more ambitious intentions than that, the casual trampolinist can pursue a most rewarding and engaging pastime. Those who want to develop expertise will need to put a lot more into the sport than that – even some theoretical study, for a knowledge of the behaviour of a body in space is necessary if acrobatics are to be finely controlled – but what can then be taken out of it is almost sublime.

The simplicity of trampolining is one of its greatest attractions. It is simple in execution and preparation, simple in its physical and mechanical requirements. Those who find little appeal in competitive team games lack no enthusiasm for trampolining, which grabs the young individual as surely as golf grabs the old.

For our familiarity with the trampoline today we probably have the Second World War to thank, but of course its roots are deeper than that. For many centuries tumblers have been using some kind of springboard from which to bounce high in the air, and nobody knows for how long the Eskimos have been tossing each other on a stretched walrus skin. It did not take circus trapeze artists long to realize that the safety net above which they worked could be put to good use for rebounding, and it was while watching this going on that the idea came to an American diving and tumbling champion, George Nissen, that the acrobatic possibilities of an apparatus specifically constructed for bouncing and rebounding were enormous.

He went home to his father's garage in Cedar Rapids, Iowa, and built a prototype, using scrap metal for the frame. He called it a 'T' Model (*trampolin* is Spanish for springboard and *trampoli* is Italian for performing on stilts). That was in 1936 and rebound tumbling, as the activity was for a long time known, had gaine sufficient foothold in the USA for trampolines to become a highly-valued part of aircrew training during the war.

By the end of it, Nissen was not alone in his absolute conviction that trampolining was going to be a world-wide sport. The first (unofficial) USA national championships were held during the Amateur Athletic Union meeting in 1947, and were won by one James Garner. The following year trampolining was accepted as a regular event in several gymnastic competitions, including that of the National Collegiate Athletic Association, but the annual championships continued to be 'unofficial' until 1954, when Robert Elliot was accepted as a real champion. The following year it was included in the Pan-American Games in Mexico, and in 1957 Nissen took a team of experts (including his wife and a former unofficial American champion, Frank La Due) to Britain and Europe, and later on to South Africa and Japan. Trampolining was beginning to cover the world.

One of that team of enthusiasts was a British diver and gymnast, Terence (Ted) Blake, who had for a long time been trying to persuade the education authority of the school at which he taught to get hold of a trampoline. Eventually they bought a second-hand one and a club was formed at Ilford, Essex. Skilful divers soon found that trampolining was a natural extension of their airborne activities, and one of the earliest experts at Ilford was young Brian Phelps, who won a bronze medal for diving at the 1960 Olympic Games. In 1959, he became the first British trampoline champion, and at the same time won the national Under-16 championship. Blake gave up schoolteaching to become managing director of the first European factory of the Nissen Trampoline Company, at Romford, Essex, and in 1959 he and four other physical education specialists became the founder members of the Amateur Gymnastic Association Trampoline Committee.

The sport now found itself in a bit of a pickle. Interest in it was growing so rapidly that other manufacturers began turning out trampolines – but the word trampoline was the registered trade mark of Nissen's company. It could not be used by anybody else, nor could it be properly used to describe a sport: accordingly, at the end of 1959 it was agreed to call the sport rebound tumbling, since so many of the movements had their origins in the ancient sporting entertainment of tumbling.

Inevitably, there were many in the long-established world of gymnastics who resented the intrusion of this new craze. They believed in particular that this mechanical aid to jumping would cause gymnasts to become lazy and lose the natural spring that they acquired only by their own efforts. Trampoline addicts strenuously denied this, and later claimed their point conclusively proved: trampolining, they said, positively developed the leg muscles, led to more powerful take-offs for gymnasts and also encouraged a far more adventurous approach to the athletic elements of the gymnastic floor exercise.

In the end, the rising enthusiasm for trampolining demanded that the two sports should grow separately. For an awkward time, there were two national bodies supervising rebound tumbling: the AGA Trampoline Committee, still its official governing body, and the British Trampoline Association, formed in 1963 to promote and develop the sport. For more than two years they lived unhappily side by side, until the British Trampoline Federation was founded in November 1965.

Meanwhile, landmarks in rebound tumbling were nevertheless achieved in Britain. The national championships drew an audience of 6,000 to the Albert Hall, London, in 1961, where they were held together with the AGA championships. In November, Britain travelled to Kiel for the first trampoline international, against West Germany. The next year, there was both the first unofficial European championships and the first European Cup tournament, both held in Germany, with the participation of Austria, Britain, Denmark, Holland, Sweden and Switzerland. The first world championships were organized by Ted Blake at the Albert Hall in March, 1964. Twelve nations sent representatives – two men and two women from each, with the exception of the USA. There too the sport was double-headed, and the AAU and the US Gymnastic Federation both insisted on sending a team.

The world championships were again held at the Albert Hall in 1965, and included the first world tumbling championships, an alliance that continued until the rise of sports acrobatics in 1977. By now, the sport was controlled world-wide by the International Trampoline Association. From 1969, the world championships were held every other year, alternating with the European championships. They were first officially held that year in Paris, where the 16-year-old British boy, Paul Luxon, surprised the sport by taking the title. He went on to win the world championship in 1970.

So much for history. What about the practicalities of the sport? First, it should go without saying that this is a potentially dangerous activity that must only be undertaken under supervision, in proper conditions and on a standard and carefully-erected trampoline. There are no set dimensions for this, but most full-size trampolines are about 12 feet by 8 feet (3.65 m × 2.45 m). The bed is usually made of a solid nylon or canvas sheet, or of woven webbing. The sheet has slower recoil (it is said to be 'heavy' to work), but is safer for beginners; a webbing bed is much livelier (and much more expensive), but needs better control by the performer, who must land evenly to avoid being thrown to one side on the rebound. Covered springs or elasticated

cables stretch the bed to its padded metal frame.

Floor space is not all you need. Indoors, advanced trampolinists need about 25 feet (7.5 m) headroom; out of doors, they need a perfectly calm day – it is surprising how little wind is required to blow you off course when you are that high above the ground. A check underneath the trampoline is necessary too: there must not be anything on the ground under the bed, not even a pair of shoes. A body coming down from even ten feet (3 m) up makes a surprisingly deep impression on the bed.

What you wear for trampolining is more important than it is for any other form of gymnastic activity. No rings, necklaces, watches, buckles, badges, not even buttons if possible; no long finger nails, no boots, no spectacles – those who cannot possibly do without them, must have elastic round the head to keep them on. Wear close-fitting clothes with long sleeves, wear socks and soft gym shoes, wear long trousers, ideally of stretch material, or tights. Those angular bits of our bodies where not much more than skin covers the bone – knees, elbows, ankles, shoulders – graze very easily. They are repeatedly thrown into contact with tough material, and the friction created can cause nasty grazes. When working on a webbed bed, the likelihood of fingers or toes being caught is high enough without increasing the risk. That is why trampolinists do everything they can to eliminate the obvious hazards of body and apparel.

However sensibly the trampolinist is turned out, it will still be a dangerous activity if there is not sufficient care and proper discipline all the time it is going on. It may seem unbelievable, but a few years ago the chief causes of trampoline accidents

21 Trampoline: seat drop

in the USA were eating, drinking and smoking – and eating includes chewing gum and sucking sweets, both of which can so easily be jolted into the windpipe. Apart from that, a trampoline is no place for fooling around. Complete concentration is needed by the performer and by the two spotters, who stand either side of the trampoline watching for deflections in flight and any other misjudgements, ready to catch or to steady the descending body. If it lands off centre, or on one foot before the other, it will rebound off centre and land again even further off centre – perhaps on the springs or the frame itself.

There is no more important skill in trampolining than that of stopping, or 'killing the bounce'. Until the novice can do that confidently, he is like someone on a bicycle without brakes. As soon as he learns how to start, he must learn how to stop. He starts by standing upright in the centre of the bed, weight evenly distributed and feet a little apart – they should be as wide as the hips. You will see him bending his knees and pushing into the bed, at the same time swinging his arms forward and up. The bed pushes back, lifting him into the air. The return (and the first lift will not be very high), must every time be to the centre of the bed, feet slightly apart, body erect but relaxed. Each time the knees must bend, pushing the feet into the bed, as the arms swing past the thighs and up again.

As soon as the beginner has the taste of rhythmic, controlled bouncing, he should practise stopping. The bounce is killed by absorbing the recoil with bent knees, but without thrusting down into the bed again. To keep balance, he will lean the upper-half of the body forward slightly, because the tendency is for a 'kill' to tip it backwards. Spreading the arms sideways helps too. At any stage in the development of a trampolinist, he must kill his bouncing as soon as he feels himself moving towards the edge of the bed: the centre is the only place from which he can safely operate.

Mounting and dismounting from a trampoline might not seem to be particularly important, but there should be nothing sloppy about those operations either. All branches of gymnastics require control and precision at all times, before and after an exercise, not just during it: the frame may be three feet (about one metre) high and the performer should stand steady on it before stepping straight out onto the bed. The neatest and steadiest dismount is to put one hand and the opposite foot on the frame and step through with the other leg.

Competitive trampolining is a challenge to the performer to perform as many different twists, turns and somersaults as he can in the ten-bounce routine allowed him, but the beginner must master the basic movements before he tries anything complicated or impressive. The preliminary exercises are not difficult, but they must be approached methodically and perfected one at a time before moving on. Once the straight bounce and stop is no longer a problem, the aspiring trampolinist will probably try a tuck, easiest and most natural of the simple movements. Incidentally, that master of technique Dennis Horne, in his splendid book *Trampolining* warns against working yourself up to an exercise with a lot of preparatory straight bounces: go straight into the movement you want, he says, so that your concentration is devoted to it.

The tuck is a position often seen in body flight activities – tumbling, vaulting, diving – and is achieved by drawing the knees tightly to the chest. The trampoline performer reaches vigorously up with his arms from take-off, helping him to a good height. Near its peak he draws the knees up and reaches down with his hands to the outside of the ankles – rated a more polished way of executing the tuck jump than grabbing the shins. The body should return to stretch for landing.

Next, a pike, the position seen even more often in every gymnasium. This is a folding of the body with legs fully extended, and the beginner, unless he is already a supple gymnast, will find it easier to work first on a piked straddle – with the legs extended, but spread apart. Another good, high jump is needed, and because of the longer, slower movement of the legs to their position parallel with the bed, it must be started earlier in the jump than was the case with the tuck. At the same time, the performer leans forward to cover his ankles with his hands, returning to the upright position for landing. For the pike without straddle, the legs should be tight together, making it a great deal harder to reach the ankles.

Twist and half-twist jumps are difficult enough to rate marks in competition, but the half-twist at least can be achieved without too much effort. Movements of the head and arms about a vertical axis cause the body to twist in the air: for a 180 degree twist, the trampolinist will not swing both his arms high over his head as he usually does, but will bring one of them across his waist. At the same time, he looks over the other shoulder, behind his raised arm, and his shoulders and hips should follow him.

The full twist (360 degrees) is a different proposition. The arms remain either straight above the head or down close to the body, and the power for the movement comes primarily from the way the performer pushed with his feet into the bed. The secondary source of twist is the rotation of the shoulders, but the degree of effort has to be determined from the start – there is no way he can add to the effort after it has begun. Nor can he stop it once it is under way, so it takes some considerable practice to work out the correct balance between the height of the bounce and the amount of twist impulse so that at the moment he lands, the trampolinist is facing the same spot he was when he took off.

One other uncomplicated movement is worth a mention, because of its particular popularity with girls: the splits jump, in which one leg is raised forward and one backward till both are parallel with the ground. The arms can either do the same, or be stretched sideways in elegant symmetry. When all those basic jumps can be executed neatly and confidently, it will be time for the ambitious novice to leave the nursery and begin the very satisfying business of dropping to the bed on other parts of his anatomy than his feet.

Seat drop

The best to begin with, because it is a natural position for the body. To find exactly the right position in which he wants to drop, the beginner should sit on the bed, legs together and stretched out in front of him, toes pointed. If the hands are put flat on the bed a few inches (centimetres) behind the seat, with the fingers pointing forwards, not sideways, he will find that his trunk is leaning back slightly. That is just how he should hit the bed. He bounces from a standing position as usual, to a good height: by the time maximum height is reached, the legs should be on the way up, about half-way to the horizontal. On the way down, the angle of legs to body continues to decrease and the arms come down behind the hips. Heels, legs, bottom, hands – all should hit the bed together.

If the trunk is upright, with the hands too near the hips, the recoil will be straight back up the same path and it will be difficult to lower the legs to the vertical again in time for the landing. By leaning back on the hands, and using them positively against the bed, there will be a slight forward thrust and the body will gently rotate round an axis through the hips, bringing the feet towards the bed again.

Knee drop

Although the take-off is from a standing position, it is again worth the novice feeling the shape of his drop before he starts bouncing. It is an absolutely upright kneel, the weight of the upper body over the knees and not the heels. For the firmest base, the heels should be together but the knees apart, hip-width. As the trampolinist rises on his jump, he lifts his heels behind him till the shins are horizontal – no further, or he is likely to sit back on them when he drops. On the rebound, beginners often try to stretch their legs downward too soon, which can cause an awkward descent.

Hands and knees drop

The landing position speaks for itself, but this time the performer can sit back on his heels a little, and the hands should not be far in front of the knees. To drop with the hands further forward will flatten the back and bring double trouble: first, there may be double recoil, from the separate impact of the hands and knees, which may buck the inexperienced out of control; secondly, by making a rigid bridge of the back and driving its two end supports onto the bed, the middle, painfully, will try to go on.

Face drop

There is a tendency for beginners to hold their faces up in this drop, away from the impact with the bed, and coaches have to work hard to banish the element of fear that causes this. The error can have entirely the opposite effect to that intended by the performer. Impact should be made with the toes, legs and body fully extended; some teach the face drop with the elbows beside the shoulders and the forearms pointing forward, either side of the head. Dennis Horne prefers the fingertips to be together, below the face, with the elbows extended sideways. Whichever way is chosen, it is vital that forearms, legs and body all hit the bed together. If the legs make contact first, as they may do if the head is lifted, recoil will come from the legs first and the face will be smacked down. It is a good idea to preface a face drop by bouncing a few times on hands and knees before shooting the legs out to the rear and tucking the forearms down. To execute the face drop properly, from the bounce, the beginner needs to start his lean forward and legs back in good time.

Back drop

Definitely the last of the basic drops to tackle. It takes a little more confidence, a little more courage, because the performer cannot see the bed until he hits it. Contact should be made with the whole of the back at once, including the seat. The legs remain clear of the bed, and so does the head. Some like the arms to be extended sideways, included in the contact area; Horne strongly recommends that they should remain folded across the chest. The correct position will be reached, he says, if as a preliminary exercise the trampolinist stands upright on the bed, feet hips-width apart, hips forward, arms folded and head forward to look at the arms. By falling backwards from that position, the ideal back drop should result. In performance, of course, it is achieved from an upright jump and ends by bouncing from the back on to the feet again.

It is very helpful to the novice if he learns at a very early stage to move smoothly and rhythmically from one drop to another. Trampoline routines must be integrated and graceful, never disjointed. By stitching neatly together his first two drops, seat to knees to seat to knees, the elementary performer gets a feeling for the flow of a routine. Knees-seat-front-back is a useful combination, though the final change often gives rise to some problems. The key is to concentrate on throwing the hips forward and up as the performer rises from his front bounce, going into the tight tuck as the body rotates in its half-back somersault. This hastens the rotation, giving the performer time to open out from the back landing.

When the elementary trampolinist is satisfied that he can cope with the basic movements, and is looking for the first touches of sophistication, he can introduce half-twists and turns to his routine.

Swivel hips

This is a half-twist in a seat drop. As the performer bounces up from his seat drop, the head and shoulders turn into a 180 degree twist, the legs drop into the standing position and rise again to a seat drop facing the other way.

Half-turntable

A similar operation on a front drop, but rather than being a half-twist, it is a half sideways-somersault. As he takes off from the face-down position, the trampolinist presses to one side with his hands and, as the body turns, brings his knees up into the tuck. The back should remain parallel with the bed throughout the turn, so that only a stretch is needed to return the body to a face drop the other way round.

Half-twist drops

At the top of the upright bounce into a face drop it is a simple matter to rotate the shoulders into a half-twist, raise the legs backwards and drop face down. For a half twist to back drop, the performer leans into a face drop on the way up, half-twists in the air, and lands in a back drop.

Competitive trampolining

It will be some time before the inexperienced gymnast is skilled and confident enough to put together a routine that will stand up to competition and serious judging, but nevertheless this is the target of all ambitious trampolinists. What will he be faced with when he comes to this level? For children the demands may be modified, but men and women will have to demonstrate a ten-bounce routine of their own choice, in which no movement is repeated. The complete routine is written down and handed to the judges, and each of the movements is awarded a difficulty rating that depends on the number of rotations (somersaults or twists) involved.

Two difficulty judges check what is actually performed against what was proposed and mark accordingly; four form judges, who are not influenced by the difficulty of the routine, award marks out of a possible ten for form and execution. The highest and lowest of their marks are discarded and the average of the other two recorded.

In individual competition, all the entrants must go through a preliminary round in which they first perform a compulsory routine of ten movements, the requirements of which are made known well in advance. They then perform their voluntary routine, after which the top ten competitors take part in the final round. This is a voluntary routine too, and though it may be entirely different from the first one (providing the judges are notified), most trampolinists repeat their original.

For team competitions, five members perform one compulsory and two voluntary routines. The method of judging is the same, but only the best four scores in each team are added together for the final result. A simplified form of judging is often used in minor competitions, when only two teams are involved: the first performer from team A is followed on the trampoline by the first from team B, and the five judges each simply hold up a card marked either A or B. The performer with the lower number of votes is 'knocked out', and at the end the winning team is that with the greater number of individual successes. In synchronized trampolining, two members of the same team jump the same routine together on two trampolines side by side and are marked for execution, difficulty (there is one voluntary and one compulsory routine) and perfection of synchronization.

Organizers of competitions try to provide ideal conditions, and expect competitors to comply absolutely with their rules. Trampolines will always be of the woven kind and will be surrounded by mats; they will also be surrounded by spotters – both sides and back and front – who are forbidden to talk to the competitors. As in most forms of gymnastics, the judges work to a precise scale of values – a deduction of 0.3, for example, for talking to a spotter (or being talked to by one); plus 0.4 for including a 360 degree somersault, 0.2 for a 360 degree twist, and so on. For failing to land on his feet after the tenth movement of his routine, a competitor loses a whole point – and so he does if he lands on his feet but falls over within three seconds.

19 Keeping Fit

Beware of thinking that gymnastics is a 'natural' sport. The amount of strength required by any serious gymnast, and even more the degree of body suppleness, is quite unnatural. However 'fit' the beginner thinks he is, however little trouble he has in running for a bus or even surviving 90 minutes' football, he will be totally unprepared for the extraordinary demands gymnastics makes on his body. There are many who come to the sport full of enthusiasm and in what seems to be excellent physical condition who never make the grade because they cannot bear the long, and sometimes tedious, process of schooling the body for the demands that will be made of it. There are others who have to be discouraged, despite their willingness to work hard and long, because of some physical deficiency – particularly sad when it is nothing more disabling than a long back that signals their incapacity to withstand gymnastic punishment.

No sport requires more absolute physical perfection than this one. If you want to see a body in good shape, look at a top-class gymnast, developed and refined in every quarter. Male or female, the advanced competitor seems to have been constructed by the gods and exercised by the angels; is capable of efforts of speed and spring beyond the reach of all but the best athletes; is as strong as a wrestler, as supple as a ballet dancer; has the poise of a prince and the courage of a human cannon ball. These are indeed unnatural attributes, and however fortunate the gymnast was in the equipment with which nature provided him, it was only by relentless work and dedication that he acquired them. It is not the business of this book to try to supplant the work of the expert coach by 'teaching' gymnastics; no sport is less suited to a standard text-book approach, nor demands more strongly instruction individually tailored; but there are preparatory areas in which it can at least make helpful suggestions to the embryonic gymnast – suggestions that might even be interesting to those whose physical activity does not take them much further than the end of the garden.

It is almost unbelievable that the average adult does so little to keep his body in reasonable working order. Long before he is half-way through his life, he has abandoned any attempt to encourage his limbs to do anything more than go through the perfunctory motions of walking, and not much of that, with a bit of garden digging thrown in if absolutely essential. A sluggish round of golf is a pleasure to many, but even there most have abandoned the exercise of carrying their clubs. The female of the species may be no more physically adventurous, but at least her pride persuades her to keep her body in acceptable shape. Not so the male, who overeats from the cradle and overdrinks shortly afterwards and seems to suffer neither anxiety nor remorse at displaying a swollen, overhanging stomach from his late twenties onwards. Concurrent with this premature deterioration, he will of course devote considerable time to polishing his car, oiling his motor-mower and mending his electric toothbrush.

Now and then an enthusiast emerges with sufficient charm and charisma to lead a nation-wide effort at keeping fit, and a certain amount of arm-swinging and knees-bending reluctantly overtakes us. What is so ridiculous is that disproportionately huge benefits are felt by a microscopic amount of time devoted to some gentle exercises at home – say ten minutes a day, or about a one-hundredth part of our waking lives, and even half that may be enough. A celebrated English football manager, Ron Saunders, simplified the matter even further when he devised – or at least publicized – one delightfully adaptable exercise that could be all things to all men according to the number of times it was repeated, the speed with which it was performed and the physical discipline the performer cared to bring to it. It is ideal for the bedroom carpet: you lie down, flat on your back, arms fully extended beyond the head, fingers and toes stretched; you get up, stand erect; you lie face down, stretched out as before. It is more exacting than it sounds. The elderly and the unfit will not want to do many of those movements, and they will do them slowly. The young gymnast can bring amplitude and grace to bear on the same exercise and turn it into a work of agile art, a delight to watch and perform. If all of us, young and old, just put a few of those under our belt before breakfast every morning, how much better, how much happier, we should feel by Christmas!

Chairman Mao had the right idea when he ordered the Chinese people to stop whatever they were doing three times a day, at the call of a bugle, and for four minutes to perform some simple, nationally-promulgated exercises. 'Fit people are healthy people, healthy people make a happy nation', he said, or words to that effect, and freedom-loving individuals of the western world find it hard to understand the contented acceptance with which the life of such a massive nation can so completely stop to allow its arms to swing and its legs to stretch. Those mass exercises are a primitive form of the group calisthenics that captivated millions between the two world wars, when disciplined demonstrations of static physical training were seen all over Europe (calisthenics: literally, strength with beauty; the art or practice of taking exercise for health).

The young gymnast in regular training will be beyond needing 'keep fit' exercises, and will be performing under supervision a warm-up routine lasting perhaps half-an-hour before he begins apparatus or mat work. This warm-up is vital to the efficiency and safety of the gymnast, whether in competition or not, and it will be designed to cater for the gymnast's particular weaknesses as well as for the specific physical tasks that he is about to meet (and they may be violent, explosive actions that it would be positively dangerous to undertake when the body is cold). The exercises suggested here could be incorporated into the first, general stages of a warm-up routine, but could equally well be used in the bedroom by the gymnast – or by his mother and father. Physical preparation of this simple kind should not make the performer tired, or hot, or out of breath. The exercises should not be performed with speed or with strain, but to produce the maximum benefit – to stretch the muscles, to flex the joints, to improve the circulation – they need to be executed with precision and gentle pressure.

Arm swings

Stand upright with arms down. Lift them both horizontally in front of you, elbows straight. Without turning your head, and keeping the arms horizontal, swing them one at a time to the side, pressing back as far as they will go and returning to the front. With both arms still held in front, raise them one at a time straight above the head and forward again to the horizontal. Lower them together to the sides again.

Next, swing the arms up again to the same front position and immediately let them swing down again together, brushing the thighs and swinging out sideways to the horizontal. Reverse the motion, swinging down to the thighs and up to the front. After a few easy, rhythmic repeats of this double-arm swing, on reaching the front position let one arm go on swinging straight up and over the head, brushing the ear if you can manage it, till it makes a full circle and comes to the front horizontal. Then drop them both into the usual double-arm swing and next time they reach the front, make the big circle with the other arm. After the next double-arm swing, circle both arms together past the ears, pushing well back.

Shoulder stretch

Stand upright, clasping the hands behind the back, or holding one thumb with the other hand. Push the arms backwards as far as possible, tipping the head and shoulders back as if trying to meet the hands. Do this slowly and insistently, not with sudden jerks. Then bend forward from the waist, keeping the hands together and pushing them as high as you can. Try the same operations sitting cross-legged on the floor.

Balance

Stand upright, feet together. Rise up on the balls of the feet as high as possible and slowly lower. Repeat several times and then do it with the feet turned out. Raise one knee, clasp it and pull it in tightly to the body. Repeat on the other leg, then one at a time raise the knee and straighten the leg. If you think you are good at that, try it while standing on the ball of the foot only.

Waist flex

Stand with feet apart, hands to the sides and fingers pointed. Dip sideways from the waist, running the hand down the legs as far as you can go, first one side, then the other. Keep the shoulders square to the front.

Again keeping the chest squarely facing front, stretch the arms above the head and clasp the hands. Keep the arms and legs straight and the heels down, and swing the body rhythmically to the left and right. Still with the feet apart, extend the arms sideways and dip down similarly left and right, this time trying to grasp the leg below the knee each time you go down.

With the feet together and hands on hips, bend forward from the waist as far as possible, then describe a big circle with your shoulders – to the right, round to the back, way out left and front again. Reverse the direction.

Sit on a stool with the arms extended sideways, anchor the hips firmly and twist the trunk well back to the left, then the right.

Stomach muscles

Sit on the floor, legs together and backs of the knees pressed to the ground. Raise the arms till they are stretched above the head, then slowly reach forward and touch your toes. Slowly lie back flat on the floor, hands by your sides. Sit up and touch your toes again (mothers and fathers are allowed to cheat a little at first, by letting the heels come up off the floor).

Lie back as before, but with the knees raised and the arms stretched out behind the head. Sit up, bringing the arms forward to the horizontal, lie back again and repeat slowly several times.

Lie flat out, arms at the sides and legs together, and raise the legs as high as you can without (if possible) lifting your shoulders. If you feel you can, follow that by raising the extended legs and the trunk at the same time, so that you sit in a 'V'.

Hips and legs

Stand upright, hands on hips. Lunge forward with each leg in turn, bending the front one and stretching the back one. This becomes an advanced exercise when performed at speed.

Stand upright, hands on hips, and do a slow knees bend, keeping the back upright. Stand straight again. Then try the knees bend with arms stretched forward, bending the trunk forward as you go down till the head is between the arms.

Lie on your side on the floor, elbow on the ground and the hand holding the head up. Slowly raise the upper leg as high as you can, keeping it straight, and slowly lower it. Repeat with both legs together, then when lying on the other side.

Finally, a few slightly more difficult exercises that the older members of the family should approach with caution. First, lie flat on the floor, face down and fully stretched.

By contracting the muscles in the region of the hips, raise both the upper body and the legs off the floor in a bow. Then, with the arms by the sides, bend the knees, grasp the ankles and pull the feet and head close together.

Lie face up on the floor, lift the legs and body into a shoulder stand (with elbows on the floor, the hands can help to support the body) and 'bicycle' with the legs.

Choose a bare wall (with paint rather than wallpaper!) and stand facing it, so that when you extend one arm with the palm vertical it is at least a foot from the wall – the further away, the harder the exercise. Lean forward so that the hand supports you, take it away and swing the other hand into its place.

Choose at least one exercise from each section, including the final one if you are fit enough, give them a fair workout once a day and at least you can be sure your moving parts will not grind to a halt for a while! Have a quiet session of yoga each day as well, take yourself off for a ten-minute jog and even the old folks will feel ridiculously fit. The young ones will feel ready to face the sterner disciplines of bridges and *battements* in the gym.

20 Results of Major Competitions since 1948

MAJOR INTERNATIONAL COMPETITIONS SINCE 1948

1948 OLYMPIC GAMES
Men

Combined exercises — Marks
1 V. Huhtanen (Fin) — 229.7
2 W. Lehmann (Switz) — 229.0
3 P. Aaltonen (Fin) — 228.8

Floor
1 F. Pataki (Hun) — 38.7
2 J. Mogyorosi-Klencs (Hun) — 38.4
3 Z. Ruzicka (Czech) — 38.1

High bar
1 J. Stalder (Switz) — 39.7
2 W. Lehmann (Switz) — 39.4
3 V. Huhtanen (Fin) — 39.2

Parallel bars
1 M. Reusch (Switz) — 39.5
2 V. Huhtanen (Fin) — 39.3
3 { C. Kipfer (Switz) / J. Stalder (Switz) } — 39.1

Pommel horse
1 { P. Aaltonen (Fin) / V. Huhtanen (Fin) / H. Savolainen (Fin) } — 38.7
2 L. Zanetti (Italy) — 38.3
3 G. Figone (Italy) — 38.2

Rings
1 K. Frei (Switz) — 39.6
2 M. Reusch (Switz) — 39.1
3 Z. Ruzicka (Czech) — 38.5

Vault
1 P. Aaltonen (Fin) — 39.1
2 O. Rove (Fin) — 39.0
3 { J. Mogyorosi-Klencs (Hun) / F. Pataki (Hun) / L. Sotornik (Czech) } — 38.5

Team
1 Finland — 1358.30
2 Switzerland — 1356.70
3 Hungary — 1330.85

Women — Marks
Team
1 Czechoslovakia — 445.45
2 Hungary — 440.55
3 USA — 422.63

1950 WORLD CHAMPIONSHIPS
Men

Combined exercises
1 W. Lehmann (Switz) — 143.30
2 M. Adatte (Switz) — 141.00
3 O. Rove (Fin) — 140.80

Floor
1 J. Stalder (Switz) — 19.25
2 E. Gebendinger (Switz) — 19.25
3 R. Dot (France) — 19.20

High bar
1 P. Aaltonen (Fin) — 19.45
2 V. Huhtanen (Fin) — 19.40
3 { W. Lehmann (Switz) / J. Stalder (Switz) } — 19.35

Parallel bars
1 H. Eugster (Switz) — 19.85
2 O. Rove (Fin) — 19.45
3 R. Dot (France) — 19.35

Pommel horse
1 J. Stalder (Switz) — 19.70
2 M. Adatte (Switz) — 19.35
3 W. Lehmann (Switz) — 19.05

Rings
1 W. Lehmann (Switz) — 19.60
2 O. Rove (Fin) — 19.30
3 H. Eugster (Switz) — 19.20

Vault
1 E. Gebendinger (Switz) — 19.45
2 O. Rove (Fin) — 19.35
3 W. Lehmann (Switz) — 19.30

Team	Marks
1 Switzerland	852.25
2 Finland	838.50
3 France	807.85

Women
Combined exercises
1 H. Rakoczy (Poland)	94.016
2 Petersen (Sweden)	91.700
3 Kolar (Austria)	91.000

Bars (or rings)
1 { Kolar (Austria) / Petersen (Sweden)	24.000
3 H. Rakoczy (Poland)	23.850

Beam
1 H. Rakoczy (Poland)	23.433
2 Nutti (Italy)	23.333
3 L. Macchini (Italy)	23.200

Floor
1 H. Rakoczy (Poland)	23.166
2 Kocis (Yugo)	23.033
3 S. Reindlowa (Poland)	23.000

Vault
1 H. Rakoczy (Poland)	23.566
2 Kolar (Austria)	23.466
3 A. Lemoine (France)	23.400

Team
1 Sweden	607.500
2 France	598.766
3 Italy	594.250

1952 OLYMPIC GAMES
Men
Combined exercises
	Marks
1 V. Chukarin (USSR)	115.70
2 G. Shaginyan (USSR)	114.95
3 J. Stalder (Switz)	114.75

Floor
1 W. Thoresson (Sweden)	19.25
2 { J. Jokiel (Poland) / T. Uesako (Japan)	19.15

High bar
1 J. Gunthard (Switz)	19.55
2 { A. Schwarzmann (Germany) / J. Stalder (Switz)	19.50

Parallel bars
1 H. Eugster (Switz)	19.65
2 V. Chukarin (USSR)	19.60
3 J. Stalder (Switz)	19.50

Pommel horse
	Marks
1 V. Chukarin (USSR)	19.50
2 { Y. Korolkov (USSR) / G. Shaginyan (USSR)	19.40

Rings
1 G. Shaginyan (USSR)	19.75
2 V. Chukarin (USSR)	19.55
3 { H. Eugster (Switz) / D. Leonkin (USSR)	19.40

Vault
1 V. Chukarin (USSR)	19.20
2 M. Takemoto (Japan)	19.15
3 { T. Ono (Japan) / T. Uesako (Japan)	19.10

Team
1 USSR	574.40
2 Switzerland	567.50
3 Finland	564.20

Women
Combined exercises
1 M. Gorokhovskaya (USSR)	76.78
2 N. Bocharova (USSR)	75.94
3 M. Korondi (Hun)	75.82

Bars
1 M. Korondi (Hun)	19.40
2 M. Gorokhovskaya (USSR)	19.26
3 A. Keleti (Hun)	19.16

Beam
1 N. Bochorova (USSR)	19.22
2 M. Gorokhovskaya (USSR)	19.13
3 M. Korondi (Hun)	19.02

Floor
1 A. Keleti (Hun)	19.36
2 M. Gorokhovskaya (USSR)	19.20
3 M. Korondi (Hun)	19.00

Vault
1 Y. Kalinchuk (USSR)	19.20
2 M. Gorokhovskaya (USSR)	19.19
3 G. Minaicheva (USSR)	19.16

Team
1 USSR	527.03
2 Hungary	520.96
3 Czechoslovakia	503.32

1954 WORLD CHAMPIONSHIPS

Men

Combined exercises

	Marks
1 { V. Muratov (USSR) / V. Chukarin (USSR)	115.45
3 G. Chaguinjane (USSR)	114.60

Floor

1 { V. Muratov (USSR) / M. Takemoto (Japan)	19.25
3 W. Thoresson (Sweden)	19.20

High bar

1 V. Muratov (USSR)	19.70
2 { H. Bantz (Germany) / B. Shakhlin (USSR)	19.40

Parallel bars

1 V. Chukarin (USSR)	19.60
2 J. Stalder (Switz)	19.55
3 { H. Bantz (Germany) / H. Eugster (Switz) / M. Takemoto (Japan)	19.40

Pommel horse

1 G. Chaguinjane (USSR)	19.30
2 J. Stalder (Switz)	19.25
3 V. Chukarin (USSR)	19.20

Rings

1 A. Azarian (USSR)	19.75
2 E. Korolkov (USSR)	19.55
3 V. Muratov (USSR)	19.50

Vault

1 L. Sotornik (Czech)	19.25
2 H. Bantz (Germany)	19.20
3 S. Diaiani (USSR)	19.10

Team

1 USSR	689.90
2 Japan	673.25
3 Switzerland	671.55

Women

Combined exercises

1 G. Roudiko (USSR)	75.68
2 E. Bosokova (Czech)	75.11
3 H. Rakoczy (Poland)	74.37

Bars

1 A. Keleti (Hun)	19.46
2 G. Roudiko (USSR)	19.33
3 H. Rakoczy (Poland)	19.20

Beam

	Marks
1 K. Tanaka (Japan)	18.89
2 E. Bosokova (Czech)	18.76
3 A. Keleti (Hun)	18.72

Floor

1 T. Manina (USSR)	19.39
2 E. Bosokova (Czech)	19.16
3 M. Gorokhovskaya (USSR)	19.12

Vault

1 { T. Manina (USSR) / A. Petterson (Sweden)	18.96
3 E. Bergren (Sweden)	18.93

Team

1 USSR	524.31
2 Hungary	518.28
3 Czechoslovakia	511.75

1955 EUROPEAN CHAMPIONSHIPS

Men

Combined exercises

	Marks
1 B. Shakhlin (USSR)	57.80
2 A. Azarian (USSR)	56.75
3 H. Bantz (Germany)	56.65

Floor

1 V. Prorok (Czech)	9.75

High bar

1 B. Shakhlin (USSR)	9.75

Parallel bar

1 { A. Azarian (USSR) / H. Bantz (Germany) / B. Shakhlin (USSR)	9.75

Pommel horse

1 B. Shakhlin (USSR)	9.75

Rings

1 A. Azarian (USSR)	9.85

Vaults

1 A. Dickhut (Germany)	9.75

1956 OLYMPIC GAMES

Men

Combined exercises

	Marks
1 V. Chukarin (USSR)	114.25
2 T. Ono (Japan)	114.20
3 Y. Titov (USSR)	113.80

Floor	Marks
1 V. Muratov (USSR)	19.20
2 { N. Aihara (Japan) / V. Chukarin (USSR) / W. Thoresson (Sweden)	19.10

High bar	
1 T. Ono (Japan)	19.60
2 Y. Titov (USSR)	19.40
3 M. Takemoto (Japan)	19.30

Parallel bars	
1 V. Chukarin (USSR)	19.20
2 M. Kubota (Japan)	19.15
3 { T. Ono (Japan) / M. Takemoto (Japan)	19.10

Pommel horse	
1 B. Shakhlin (USSR)	19.25
2 T. Ono (Japan)	19.20
3 V. Chukarin (USSR)	19.10

Rings	
1 A. Azarian (USSR)	19.35
2 V. Muratov (USSR)	19.15
3 { M. Kubota (Japan) / M. Takemoto (Japan)	19.10

Vault	
1 { H. Bantz (Germany) / V. Muratov (USSR)	18.85
3 Y. Titov (USSR)	18.75

Team	
1 USSR	568.25
2 Japan	566.40
3 Finland	555.95

Women
Combined exercises

1 L. Latynina (USSR)	74.933
2 A. Keleti (Hun)	74.633
3 S. Muratova (USSR)	74.466

Bars	
1 A. Keleti (Hun)	18.966
2 L. Latynina (USSR)	18.833
3 S. Muratova (USSR)	18.800

Beam	
1 A. Keleti (Hun)	18.800
2 { E. Bosokova (Czech) / T. Manina (USSR)	18.633

Floor	Marks
1 { A. Keleti (Hun) / L. Latynina (USSR)	18.733
3 E. Leustean (Rom)	18.700

Vault	
1 L. Latynina (USSR)	18.833
2 T. Manina (USSR)	18.800
3 { A. S. Colling (Sweden) / O. Tass (Hun)	18.733

Team	
1 USSR	444.80
2 Hungary	443.50
3 Romania	438.20

1957 EUROPEAN CHAMPIONSHIPS
Men

Combined exercises	Marks
1 Blume (Spain)	57.40
2 Y. Titov (USSR)	56.85
3 M. Benker (Switz)	55.90

Floor	
1 W. Thoresson (Sweden)	19.55
2 N. Stuart (GB)	19.20
3 H. Schmitt (FGR)	19.10

High bar	
1 J. Gunthard (Switz)	19.55
2 Blume (Spain)	19.45
3. Y. Titov (USSR)	19.20

Parallel bars	
1 { J. Gunthard (Switz) / Blume (Spain)	19.15
3 M. Benker (Switz)	19.10

Pommel horse	
1 Blume (Spain)	19.20
2 M. Benker (Switz)	19.00
3 I. Caklec (Yugo)	18.60

Rings	
1 Blume (Spain)	19.65
2 Y. Titov (USSR)	19.55
3 K. Suomeni (Fin)	19.45

Vault	
1 Y. Titov (USSR)	19.15
2 R. Csanyi (Hun)	18.85
3 W. Thoresson (Sweden)	18.80

Women

Combined exercises	Marks
1 L. Latynina (USSR)	38.465
2 E. Teodorescu (Romania)	37.798
3 S. Iovan (Romania)	37.599

Bars	
1 L. Latynina (USSR)	19.466
2 E. Teodorescu (Romania)	19.232
3 E. Bosokova (Czech)	19.066

Beam	
1 L. Latynina (USSR)	19.000
2 S. Iovan (Romania)	18.999
3 T. Manina (USSR)	18.733

Floor	
1 L. Latynina (USSR)	19.332
2 E. Teodorescu (Romania)	19.266
3 E. Bosokova (Czech)	19.199

Vault	
1 L. Latynina (USSR)	19.299
2 T. Manina (USSR)	18.933
3 S. Iovan (Romania)	18.733

1958 WORLD CHAMPIONSHIPS

Men

Combined exercises	Marks
1 B. Shakhlin (USSR)	116.05
2 T. Ono (Japan)	115.60
3 Y. Titov (USSR)	115.45

Floor	
1 M. Takemoto (Japan)	19.55
2 T. Ono (Japan)	19.50
3 Y. Titov (USSR)	19.40

High bar	
1 B. Shakhlin (USSR)	19.575
2 A. Azarian (USSR)	19.35
3 { Y. Titov (USSR) / M. Takemoto (Japan) }	19.30

Parallel bars	
1 B. Shakhlin (USSR)	19.65
2 Takemoto (Japan)	19.15
3 T. Ono (Japan)	19.125

Pommel horse	
1 B. Shakhlin (USSR)	19.55
2 P. Stolbov (USSR)	19.375
3 M. Cerar (Yugo)	19.35

Rings	Marks
1 A. Azarian (USSR)	19.875
2 N. Aihara (Japan)	19.475
3 Y. Titov (USSR)	19.455

Vault	
1 Y. Titov (USSR)	19.35
2 M. Takemoto (Japan)	19.15
3 T. Ono (Japan)	19.125

Team	
1 USSR	575.45
2 Japan	572.60
3 Czechoslovakia	549.30

Women

Combined exercises	
1 L. Latynina (USSR)	77.464
2 E. Bosokova (Czech)	76.332
3 T. Manina (USSR)	76.167

Bars	
1 L. Latynina (USSR)	19.499
2 E. Bosokova (Czech)	19.300
3 P. Astakhova (USSR)	19.199

Beam	
1 L. Latynina (USSR)	19.399
2 S. Muratova (USSR)	19.099
3 K. Tonaka (Japan)	19.066

Floor	
1 E. Bosokova (Czech)	19.400
2 L. Latynina (USSR)	19.333
3 K. Tonaka (Japan)	19.199

Vault	
1 L. Latynina (USSR)	19.233
2 { L. Kalina (USSR) / T. Manina (USSR) / S. Muratova (USSR) }	19.100

Team	
1 USSR	381.620
2 Czechoslovakia	371.855
3 Romania	367.020

1959 EUROPEAN CHAMPIONSHIPS

Men

Combined exercises	Marks
1 Y. Titov (USSR)	57.85
2 P. Stolbov (USSR)	56.30
3 P. Furst (FGR)	55.45

Floor	Marks
1 E. Fivian (Switz)	19.20
2 W. Thoresson (Sweden)	19.15
3 Y. Titov (USSR)	18.90

High bar

1 P. Stolbov (USSR)	19.55
2 Y. Titov (USSR)	19.35
3 { J. Cronstedt (Sweden) / O. Kestola (Fin)	19.05

Parallel bars

1 Y. Titov (USSR)	19.15
2 F. Danis (Czech)	18.90
3 P. Stolbov (USSR)	18.80

Pommel horse

1 Y. Titov (USSR)	19.25
2 E. Eckmann (Fin)	18.85
3 P. Furst (FGR)	18.80

Rings

1 Y. Titov (USSR)	19.60
2 P. Stolbov (USSR)	19.50
3 { V. Kapsazov (Bulg) / O. Kestola (Fin)	19.25

Vault

1 { W. Thoresson (Sweden) / Y. Titov (USSR)	19.30
3 E. Fivian (Switz)	19.10

Women
Combined exercises

1 N. Kot (Poland)	37.833
2 E. Teodorescu (Romania)	37.767
3 S. Iovan (Romania)	37.401

Bars

1 P. Astakhova (USSR)	19.467
2 E. Teodorescu (Romania)	19.200
3 I. Fost (GDR)	19.034

Beam

1 V. Caslavska (Czech)	19.166
2 S. Iovan (Romania)	18.867
3 N. Kot (Poland)	18.800

Floor

1 P. Astakhova (USSR)	19.400
2 T. Manina (USSR)	19.200
3 E. Bosokova (Czech)	19.100

Vault	Marks
1 N. Kot (Poland)	19.010
2 V. Caslavska (Czech)	18.967
3 I. Fost (GDR)	18.934

1960 OLYMPIC GAMES
Men

Combined exercises	Marks
1 B. Shakhlin (USSR)	115.95
2 T. Ono (Japan)	115.90
3 Y. Titov (USSR)	115.60

Floor

1 N. Aihara (Japan)	19.45
2 Y. Titov (USSR)	19.325
3 F. Menichelli (Italy)	19.275

High bar

1 T. Ono (Japan)	19.60
2 M. Takemoto (Japan)	19.52
3 B. Shakhlin (USSR)	19.475

Parallel bars

1 B. Shakhlin (USSR)	19.40
2 G. Carminucci (Italy)	19.375
3 T. Ono (Japan)	19.35

Pommel horse

1 { E. Ekman (Fin) / B. Shakhlin (USSR)	19.375
3 S. Tsurumi (Japan)	19.15

Rings

1 A. Azarian (USSR)	19.725
2 B. Shakhlin (USSR)	19.50
3 { V. Kapsazov (Bulg) / T. Ono (Japan)	19.425

Vault

1 { T. Ono (Japan) / B. Shakhlin (USSR)	19.35
3 V. Portnoi (USSR)	19.225

Team

1 Japan	575.20
2 USSR	572.70
3 Italy	559.05

Women
Combined exercises

1 L. Latynina (USSR)	77.031
2 S. Muratova (USSR)	76.696
3 P. Astakhova (USSR)	76.164

Bars	**Marks**
1 P. Astakhova (USSR)	19.616
2 L. Latynina (USSR)	19.416
3 T. Lyukhina (USSR)	19.399

Beam	
1 E. Bosokova (Czech)	19.283
2 L. Latynina (USSR)	19.233
3 S. Muratova (USSR)	19.232

Floor	
1 Latynina (USSR)	19.583
2 P. Astakhova (USSR)	19.532
3 T. Lyukhina (USSR)	19.449

Vault	
1 M. Nikolaeva (USSR)	19.316
2 S. Muratova (USSR)	19.049
3 L. Latynina (USSR)	19.016

Team	
1 USSR	382.32
2 Czechoslovakia	373.323
3 Romania	372.053

1961 EUROPEAN CHAMPIONSHIPS

Men

Combined exercises	**Marks**
1 M. Cerar (Yugo)	58.05
2 Y. Titov (USSR)	56.85
3 G. Carminucci (Italy)	56.65

Floor	
1 F. Menichelli (Italy)	19.45
2 V. Leontiev (USSR)	19.35
3 M. Cerar (Yugo)	19.30

High bar	
1 Y. Titov (USSR)	19.50
2 R. Csanyi (Hun)	19.45
3 O. Kestola (Fin)	19.35

Parallel bars	
1 M. Cerar (Yugo)	19.55
2 V. Leontiev (USSR)	19.00
3 {G. Carminucci (Italy) / F. Menichelli (Italy)}	18.95

Pommel horse	
1 M. Cerar (Yugo)	19.60
2 {P. Furst (FGR) / V. Leontiev (USSR)}	18.65

Rings	**Marks**
1 {M. Cerar (Yugo) / V. Kapsazov (Bulg) / Y. Titov (USSR)}	19.25

Vault	
1 G. Carminucci (Italy)	19.35
2 F. Menichelli (Italy)	19.25
3 {M. Cerar (Yugo) / E. Fivian (Switz) / W. Thoresson (Sweden)}	19.20

Women

Combined exercises	
1 L. Latynina (USSR)	38.50
2 P. Astakhova (USSR)	38.20
3 {V. Caslavska (Czech) / I. Fost (GDR)}	38.15

Bars	
1 P. Astakhova (USSR)	19.400
2 L. Latynina (USSR)	19.250
3 I. Fost (GDR)	19.100

Beam	
1 P. Astakhova (USSR)	19.433
2 L. Latynina (USSR)	19.317
3 I. Fost (GDR)	19.183

Floor	
1 L. Latynina (USSR)	19.400
2 P. Astakhova (USSR)	19.267
3 V. Caslavska (Czech)	19.217

Vault	
1 U. Starke (GDR)	19.350
2 I. Fost (GDR)	19.083
3 N. Kot (Poland)	19.050

1962 WORLD CHAMPIONSHIPS

Men

Combined exercises	**Marks**
1 Y. Titov (USSR)	115.65
2 Y. Endo (Japan)	115.50
3 B. Shakhlin (USSR)	115.20

Floor	
1 {N. Aihara (Japan) / Y. Endo (Japan)}	19.50
3 F. Menichelli (Italy)	19.450

High bar	
1 T. Ono (Japan)	19.675
2 {Y. Endo (Japan) / P. Stolbov (USSR)}	19.625

Parallel bars	Marks
1 M. Cerar (Yugo)	19.625
2 B. Shakhlin (USSR)	19.600
3 Y. Endo (Japan)	19.500

Pommel horse	
1 M. Cerar (Yugo)	19.750
2 B. Shakhlin (USSR)	19.375
3 { T. Mitsukuri (Japan) / Yu Lieh-feng (China) }	19.300

Rings	
1 Y. Titov (USSR)	19.550
2 { B. Shakhlin (USSR) / Y. Endo (Japan) }	19.425

Vault	
1 P. Krbec (Czech)	19.550
2 H. Yamashita (Japan)	19.350
3 { Y. Endo (Japan) / B. Shakhlin (USSR) }	19.225

Team	
1 Japan	574.65
2 USSR	573.15
3 Czechoslovakia	561.50

Women
Combined exercises	
1 L. Latynina (USSR)	78.030
2 V. Caslavska (Czech)	77.732
3 I. Pervuschina (USSR)	77.465

Bars	
1 I. Pervuschina (USSR)	19.566
2 E. Bosokova (Czech)	19.466
3 L. Latynina (USSR)	19.449

Beam	
1 E. Bosokova (Czech)	19.499
2 L. Latynina (USSR)	19.416
3 { A. Ducza (Hun) / K. Ikeda (Japan) }	19.366

Floor	
1 L. Latynina (USSR)	19.716
2 I. Pervuschina (USSR)	19.616
3 V. Caslavska (Czech)	19.550

Vault	
1 V. Caslavska (Czech)	19.649
2 L. Latynina (USSR)	19.632
3 T. Manina (USSR)	19.549

Team	Marks
1 USSR	384.988
2 Czechoslovakia	382.590
3 Japan	379.523

1963 EUROPEAN CHAMPIONSHIPS
Men
Combined exercises	Marks
1 M. Cerar (Yugo)	57.75
2 B. Shakhlin (USSR)	57.65
3 V. Kerdemelidi (USSR)	57.45

Floor	
1 F. Menichelli (Italy)	19.55
2 V. Kerdemelidi (USSR)	19.45
3 M. Cerar (Yugo)	19.15

High bar	
1 { M. Cerar (Yugo) / B. Shakhlin (USSR) }	19.70
3 V. Kerdemelidi (USSR)	19.50

Parallel bars	
1 G. Carminucci (Italy)	19.40
2 B. Shakhlin (USSR)	19.25
3 F. Menichelli (Italy)	19.20

Pommel horse	
1 M. Cerar (Yugo)	19.65
2 V. Kerdemelidi (USSR)	19.40
3 B. Shakhlin (USSR)	19.35

Rings	
1 { M. Cerar (Yugo) / V. Kapsazov (Bulg) / B. Shakhlin (USSR) }	19.25

Vault	
1 P. Krbec (Czech)	19.55
2 M. Cerar (Yugo)	19.05
3 V. Kerdemelidi (USSR) / M. Srot (Yugo)	18.95

Women
Combined exercises	
1 M. Bilic (Yugo)	37.232
2 S. Egman (Sweden)	37.131
3 E. Rydell (Sweden)	36.966

Bars	
1 T. Belmer (Holland)	18.766
2 K. Kocis (Yugo)	18.733
3 S. Egman (Sweden)	18.566

Beam	Marks
1 E. Rydell (Sweden)	19.033
2 K. Kocis (Yugo)	18.500
3 M. Bilic (Yugo)	18.400

Floor	
1 M. Bilic (Yugo)	18.932
2 S. Egman (Sweden)	18.899
3 K. Kocis (Yugo)	18.766

Vault	
1 S. Egman (Sweden)	19.032
2 T. Belmer (Holland)	18.799
3 J. Viersta (Holland)	18.732

1964 OLYMPIC GAMES

Men

Combined exercises	Marks
1 Y. Endo (Japan)	115.95
2 { V. Lisitski (USSR) / B. Shakhlin (USSR) / S. Tsurumi (Japan)	115.40

Floor	
1 F. Menichelli (Italy)	19.45
2 V. Lisitski (USSR)	19.35
3 Y. Endo (Japan)	19.35

High bar	
1 B. Shakhlin (USSR)	19.625
2 Y. Titov (USSR)	19.55
3 M. Cerar (Yugo)	19.50

Parallel bars	
1 Y. Endo (Japan)	19.675
2 S. Tsurumi (Japan)	19.45
3 F. Menichelli (Italy)	19.35

Pommel horse	
1 M. Cerar (Yugo)	19.525
2 S. Tsurumi (Japan)	19.325
3 Y. Tsapenko (USSR)	19.20

Rings	
1 T. Hayata (Japan)	19.475
2 F. Menichelli (Italy)	19.425
3 B. Shakhlin (USSR)	19.40

Vault	
1 H. Yamashita (Japan)	19.660
2 V. Lisitski (USSR)	19.325
3 H. Rantakari (Fin)	19.30

Team	
1 Japan	577.95
2 USSR	575.45
3 GDR	565.10

Women

Combined exercises	Marks
1 V. Caslavska (Czech)	77.564
2 L. Latynina (USSR)	76.998
3 P. Astakhova (USSR)	76.965

Bars	
1 P. Astakhova (USSR)	19.332
2 K. Makray (Hun)	19.216
3 L. Latynina (USSR)	19.199

Beam	
1 V. Caslavska (Czech)	19.449
2 T. Manina (USSR)	19.399
3 L. Latynina (USSR)	19.382

Floor	
1 L. Latynina (USSR)	19.599
2 P. Astakhova (USSR)	19.50
3 A. Janosi (Hun)	19.30

Vault	
1 V. Caslavska (Czech)	19.483
2 L. Latynina (USSR)	19.283
3 B. Radochla (GDR)	19.283

Team	
1 USSR	380.890
2 Czechoslovakia	379.989
3 Japan	377,889

1965 EUROPEAN CHAMPIONSHIPS

Men

Combined exercises	Marks
1 F. Menichelli (Italy)	57.55
2 V. Lisitski (USSR)	57.50
3 S. Diamidov (USSR)	56.95

Floor	
1 F. Menichelli (Italy)	19.50
2 { M. Cerar (Yugo) / V. Lisitski (USSR)	18.95

High bar	
1 F. Menichelli (Italy)	19.55
2 V. Lisitski (USSR)	19.40
3 S. Diamidov (USSR)	19.35

Parallel bars	
1 M. Cerar (Yugo)	19.50
2 F. Menichelli (Italy)	19.35
3 { S. Diamidov (USSR) / E. Koppe (GDR)	19.25

Pommel horse	Marks
1 V. Lisitski (USSR)	19.35
2 M. Cerar (Yugo)	19.25
3 S. Diamidov (USSR) / O. Laiho (Fin)	19.20

Rings	
1 V. Lisitski (USSR) / F. Menichelli (Italy)	19.35
3 M. Cerar (Yugo)	19.25

Vault	
1 V. Lisitski (USSR)	19.10
2 G. Adamov (Bulg) / R. Heinonen (Fin) / A. Storhaug (Norway)	18.95

Women
Combined exercises

1 V. Caslavska (Czech)	38.899
2 L. Latynina (USSR)	38.198
3 B. Radochla (GDR)	37.998

Bars

1 V. Caslavska (Czech)	19.633
2 L. Latynina (USSR)	19.299
3 M. Karaschka (Bulg)	19.299

Beam

1 V. Caslavska (Czech)	19.433
2 L. Latynina (USSR)	19.299
3 L. Petrik (USSR) / B. Radochla (GDR)	19.099

Floor

1 V. Caslavska (Czech)	19.333
2 L. Latynina (USSR) / B. Radochla (GDR)	19.066

Vault

1 V. Caslavska (Czech)	19.750
2 U. Starke (GDR)	19.500
3 L. Latynina (USSR)	19.366

1966 WORLD CHAMPIONSHIPS

Men

Combined exercises	Marks
1 M. Voronin (USSR)	116.15
2 S. Tsurumi (Japan)	115.25
3 A. Nakayama (Japan)	114.95

Floor

1 A. Nakayama (Japan)	19.400
2 Y. Endo (Japan)	19.375
3 F. Menichelli (Italy)	19.300

High bar	Marks
1 A. Nakayama (Japan)	19.675
2 Y. Endo (Japan)	19.600
3 T. Mitsukuri (Japan)	19.425

Parallel bars

1 S. Diamidov (USSR)	19.550
2 M. Voronin (USSR)	19.400
3 M. Cerar (Yugo)	19.350

Pommel horse

1 M. Cerar (Yugo)	19.525
2 M. Voronin (USSR)	19.325
3 T. Kato (Japan)	19.125

Rings

1 M. Voronin (USSR)	19.750
2 A. Nakayama (Japan)	19.500
3 F. Menichelli (Italy)	19.475

Vault

1 H. Matsuda (Japan)	19.425
2 T. Kato (Japan)	19.325
3 A. Nakayama (Japan)	19.050

Team

1 Japan	575.15
2 USSR	570.90
3 GDR	561.00

Women
Combined exercises

1 V. Caslavska (Czech)	78.298
2 N. Kuchinskaya (USSR)	78.097
3 K. Ikeda (Japan)	76.997

Bars

1 N. Kuchinskaya (USSR)	19.616
2 K. Ikeda (Japan)	19.566
3 T. Mitsukuri (Japan)	19.516

Beam

1 N. Kuchinskaya (USSR)	19.650
2 V. Caslavska (Czech)	19.333
3 L. Petrik (USSR)	19.250

Floor

1 N. Kuchinskaya (USSR)	19.733
2 V. Caslavska (Czech)	19.683
3 Z. Druginina (USSR)	19.666

Vault

1 V. Caslavska (Czech)	19.583
2 E. Zuchold (GDR)	19.399
3 N. Kuchinskaya (USSR)	19.316

Team	Marks
1 Czechoslovakia	383.625
2 USSR	383.587
3 Japan	380.923

1967 EUROPEAN CHAMPIONSHIPS

Men

Combined exercises	Marks
1 M. Voronin (USSR)	58.00
2 V. Lisitski (USSR)	57.30
3 F. Menichelli (Italy)	57.25

Floor

1 L. Laine (Fin)	19.15
2 F. Menichelli (Italy)	19.10
3 N. Kubica (Poland)	18.80

High bar

1 V. Lisitski (USSR)	19.45
2 M. Voronin (USSR)	19.40
3 { M. Cerar (Yugo) / F. Menichelli (Italy)	19.15

Parallel bars

1 M. Voronin (USSR)	19.40
2 F. Menichelli (Italy)	19.30
3 G. Carminucci (Italy)	19.20

Pommel horse

1 M. Voronin (USSR)	19.55
2 M. Cerar (Yugo)	19.20
3 G. Dietrich (GDR)	18.90

Rings

1 { V. Lisitski (USSR) / M. Voronin (USSR)	19.40
3 N. Kubica (Poland)	19.10

Vault

1 V. Lisitski (USSR)	19.20
2 G. Adamov (Bulg)	18.775
3 G. Dietrich (GDR)	18.175

Women

Combined Exercises

1 V. Caslavska (Czech)	38.965
2 Z. Druginina (USSR)	38.533
3 M. Kraycirovaj (Czech)	38.199

Bars

1 V. Caslavska (Czech)	19.199
2 K. Janz (GDR)	19.166
3 M. Kraycirovaj (Czech)	19.066

Beam

	Marks
1 V. Caslavska (Czech)	19.833
2 N. Kuchinskaya (USSR)	19.666
3 Z. Druginina (USSR)	19.499

Floor

1 V. Caslavska (Czech)	19.866
2 N. Kuchinskaya (USSR)	19.733
3 Z. Druginina (USSR)	19.666

Vault

1 V. Caslavska (Czech)	19.733
2 E. Zuchold (GDR)	19.533
3 K. Janz (GDR)	19.333

1968 OLYMPIC GAMES

Men

Combined exercises	Marks
1 S. Kato (Japan)	115.90
2 M. Voronin (USSR)	115.85
3 A. Nakayama (Japan)	115.65

Floor

1 S. Kato (Japan)	19.475
2 A. Nakayama (Japan)	19.40
3 T. Kato (Japan)	19.275

High bar

1 { A. Nakayama (Japan) / M. Voronin (USSR)	19.550
3 E. Kenmotsu (Japan)	19.375

Parallel bars

1 A. Nakayama (Japan)	19.475
2 M. Voronin (USSR)	19.425
3 V. Klimenko (USSR)	19.225

Pommel horse

1 M. Cerar (Yugo)	19.325
2 O. Laiho (Fin)	19.225
3 M. Voronin (USSR)	19.20

Rings

1 A. Nakayama (Japan)	19.45
2 M. Voronin (USSR)	19.325
3 S. Kato (Japan)	19.225

Vault

1 M. Voronin (USSR)	19.000
2 Y. Endo (Japan)	18.95
3 S. Diomidov (USSR)	18.925

Team

1 Japan	575.90
2 USSR	571.10
3 GDR	557.15

Women

Combined exercises	Marks
1 V. Caslavska (Czech)	78.25
2 Z. Voronina (USSR)	76.85
3 N. Kuchinskaya (USSR)	76.75

Bars

1 V. Caslavska (Czech)	19.65
2 K. Janz (GDR)	19.50
3 Z. Voronina (USSR)	19.425

Beam

1 N. Kuchinskaya (USSR)	19.65
2 V. Caslavska (Czech)	19.575
3 L. Petrik (USSR)	19.25

Floor

1 { V. Caslavska (Czech) / L. Petrik (USSR)	19.675
3 N. Kuchinskaya (USSR)	19.65

Vault

1 V. Caslavska (Czech)	19.775
2 E. Zuchold (GDR)	19.625
3 Z. Voronina (USSR)	19.50

Team

1 USSR	382.85
2 Czechoslovakia	382.20
3 GDR	379.10

1969 EUROPEAN CHAMPIONSHIPS

Men

Combined exercises	Marks
1 M. Voronin (USSR)	57.45
2 V. Klimenko (USSR)	57.00
3 N. Kubica (Poland)	56.85

Floor

1 R. Christow (Bulg)	19.20
2 V. Lisitski (USSR)	18.85
3 S. Kubica (Poland)	18.80

High bar

1 { V. Klimenko (USSR) / V. Lisitski (USSR)	19.25
3 M. Cerar (Yugo)	19.20

Parallel bars

1 M. Voronin (USSR)	19.05
2 { M. Cerar (Yugo) / V. Klimenko (USSR)	18.95

Pommel horse

	Marks
1 { M. Cerar (Yugo) / W. Kubica (Poland)	19.50
3 M. Voronin (USSR)	19.45

Rings

1 M. Voronin (USSR)	19.50
2 { V. Klimenko (USSR) / N. Kubica (Poland)	19.30

Vault

1 V. Klimenko (USSR)	18.65
2 { N. Kubica (Poland) / M. Voronin (USSR)	18.55

Women

Combined exercises	
1 K. Janz (GDR)	38.65
2 O. Karassova (USSR)	38.10
3 { L. Tourischeva (USSR) / E. Zuchold (GDR)	37.90

Bars

1 K. Janz (GDR)	19.65
2 O. Karassova (USSR)	19.45
3 L. Tourischeva (USSR)	19.40

Beam

1 K. Janz (GDR)	19.05
2 O. Karassova (USSR)	18.95
3 J. Kostalova (Czech)	18.75

Floor

1 O. Karassova (USSR)	19.45
2 K. Janz (GDR)	19.40
3 { J. Kostalova (Czech) / L. Tourischeva (USSR)	19.10

Vault

1 K. Janz (GDR)	19.70
2 E. Zuchold (GDR)	19.45
3 O. Karassova (USSR)	19.40

1970 WORLD CHAMPIONSHIPS

Men

Combined exercises	Marks
1 E. Kenmotsu (Japan)	115.05
2 M. Tsukahara (Japan)	113.85
3 A. Nakayama (Japan)	113.80

Floor

1 A. Nakayama (Japan)	19.025
2 E. Kenmotsu (Japan)	18.975
3 T. Kato (Japan)	18.900

High bar	Marks
1 E. Kenmotsu (Japan)	19.475
2 A. Nakayama (Japan)	19.375
3 { T. Hayata (Japan) / K. Koste (GDR)	19.350

Parallel bars	
1 A. Nakayama (Japan)	19.400
2 { E. Kenmotsu (Japan) / M. Voronin (USSR)	19.250

Pommel horse	
1 M. Cerar (Yugo)	19.375
2 E. Kenmotsu (Japan)	19.325
3 V. Klimenko (USSR)	19.050

Rings	
1 A. Nakayama (Japan)	19.400
2 M. Tsukahara (Japan)	19.250
3 M. Voronin (USSR)	19.225

Vault	
1 M. Tsukahara (Japan)	19.125
2 V. Klimenko (USSR)	19.000
3 T. Kato (Japan)	18.600

Team	
1 Japan	571.10
2 USSR	564.35
3 GDR	553.15

Women

Combined exercises	
1 L. Tourischeva (USSR)	77.05
2 E. Zuchold (GDR)	76.45
3 Z. Voronina (USSR)	76.15

Bars	
1 K. Janz (GDR)	19.550
2 L. Tourischeva (USSR)	19.450
3 Z. Voronina (USSR)	19.300

Beam	
1 E. Zuchold (GDR)	19.200
2 C. Rigby (USA)	19.050
3 { L. Petrik (USSR) / C. Schmitt (GDR)	18.900

Floor	
1 L. Tourischeva (USSR)	19.650
2 O. Karassova (USSR)	19.525
3 Z. Voronina (USSR)	19.375

Vault	Marks
1 E. Zuchold (GDR)	19.450
2 K. Janz (GDR)	19.350
3 { L. Burda (USSR) / L. Tourischeva (USSR)	19.300

Team	
1 USSR	380.65
2 GDR	377.75
3 Czechoslovakia	371.90

1971 EUROPEAN CHAMPIONSHIPS
Men

Combined exercises	Marks
1 V. Klimenko (USSR)	56.90
2 M. Voronin (USSR)	56.70
3 N. Andrianov (USSR)	56.25

Floor	
1 R. Christov (Bulg)	19.10
2 J. Gines (Spain)	18.75
3 N. Andrianov (USSR)	18.70

High bar	
1 K. Koste (GDR)	19.05
2 M. Voronin (USSR)	18.95
3 R. Hurzeler (Switz)	18.85

Parallel bars	
1 G. Carminucci (Italy)	18.85
2 { N. Andrianov (USSR) / K. Koste (GDR) / M. Voronin (USSR)	18.80

Pommel horse	
1 N. Andrianov (USSR)	18.90
2 M. Brehme (GDR)	18.75
3 M. Voronin (USSR)	18.70

Rings	
1 M. Voronin (USSR)	19.25
2 N. Andrianov (USSR)	18.80
3 A. Szajna (Poland)	18.70

Vault	
1 N. Andrianov (USSR)	18.75
2 A. Szajna (Poland)	18.675
3 K. Koste (GDR)	18.50

Women

Combined exercises	
1 { L. Tourischeva (USSR) / T. Lazakovitch (USSR)	38.85
2 E. Zuchold (GDR)	38.30

Bars	Marks
1 T. Lazakovitch (USSR)	19.35
2 L. Tourischeva (USSR)	19.20
3 A. Hellmann (GDR)	19.00

Beam	
1 T. Lazakovitch (USSR)	19.20
2 L. Tourischeva (USSR)	19.15
3 E. Zuchold (GDR)	19.00

Floor	
1 L. Tourischeva (USSR)	19.65
2 T. Lazakovitch (USSR)	19.60
3 E. Zuchold (GDR)	19.25

Vault	
1 L. Tourischeva (USSR)	19.60
2 T. Lazakovitch (USSR)	19.55
3 E. Zuchold (GDR)	19.50

1972 OLYMPIC GAMES

Men

Combined exercises	Marks
1 S. Kato (Japan)	114.65
2 E. Kenmotsu (Japan)	114.575
3 A. Nakayama (Japan)	114.325

Floor	
1 N. Andrianov (USSR)	19.175
2 A. Nakayama (Japan)	19.125
3 S. Kasamatsu (Japan)	19.025

High bar	
1 M. Tsukahara (Japan)	19.725
2 S. Kato (Japan)	19.525
3 S. Kasamatsu (Japan)	19.45

Parallel bars	
1 S. Kato (Japan)	19.475
2 S. Kasamatsu (Japan)	19.375
3 E. Kenmotsu (Japan)	19.25

Pommel horse	
1 V. Klimenko (USSR)	19.125
2 S. Kato (Japan)	19.00
3 E. Kenmotsu (Japan)	18.95

Rings	
1 A. Nakayama (Japan)	19.35
2 M. Voronin (USSR)	19.275
3 M. Tsukahara (Japan)	19.225

Vault	
1 K. Koste (GDR)	18.85
2 V. Klimenko (USSR)	18.825
3 N. Andrianov (USSR)	18.80

Team	Marks
1 Japan	571.25
2 USSR	564.05
3 GDR	557.15

Women

Combined exercises	
1 L. Tourischeva (USSR)	77.025
2 K. Janz (GDR)	76.875
3 T. Lazakovitch (USSR)	76.85

Bars	
1 K. Janz (GDR)	19.675
2 { O. Korbut (USSR) / E. Zuchold (GDR) }	19.45

Beam	
1 O. Korbut (USSR)	19.40
2 T. Lazakovitch (USSR)	19.375
3 K. Janz (GDR)	18.975

Floor	
1 O. Korbut (USSR)	19.575
2 L. Tourischeva (USSR)	19.550
3 T. Lazakovitch (USSR)	19.450

Vault	
1 K. Janz (GDR)	19.525
2 E. Zuchold (GDR)	19.275
3 L. Tourischeva (USSR)	19.25

Team	
1 USSR	380.50
2 GDR	376.55
3 Hungary	368.25

1973 EUROPEAN CHAMPIONSHIPS

Men

Combined exercises	Marks
1 V. Klimenko (USSR)	56.55
2 N. Andrianov (USSR)	56.30
3 K. Koste (GDR)	55.70

Floor	
1 N. Andrianov (USSR)	18.85
2 K. Klimenko (USSR)	18.80
3 K. Koste (GDR)	18.45

High bar	
1 { E. Gienger (FGR) / K. Koste (GDR) }	19.25
3 W. Thune (GDR)	19.20

Parallel bars	
1 V. Klimenko (USSR)	18.95
2 { N. Andrianov (USSR) / M. Nissinen (Fin) }	18.75

Pommel horse	Marks
1 Z. Magyar (Hun)	19.05
2 W. Kubica (Poland)	18.80
3 V. Klimenko (USSR)	18.75

Rings

1 V. Klimenko (USSR)	18.80
2 {N. Andrianov (USSR) / D. Grecu (Romania)	18.75

Vaults

1 N. Andrianov (USSR)	18.70
2 A. Szajna (Poland)	18.65
3 I. Molnar (Hun)	18.15

Women
Combined exercises

1 L. Tourischeva (USSR)	38.10
2 O. Korbut (USSR)	37.65
3 K. Gerschau (GDR)	37.40

Bars

1 L. Tourischeva (USSR)	19.30
2 A. Hellmann (GDR)	19.25
3 A. Goreac (Romania)	18.95

Beam

1 L. Tourischeva (USSR)	19.10
2 A. Goreac (Romania)	18.85
3 A. Grigoras (Romania)	18.75

Floor

1 L. Tourischeva (USSR)	18.90
2 K. Gerschau (GDR)	18.80
3 A. Goreac (Romania)	18.75

Vault

1 {A. Hellmann (GDR) / L. Tourischeva (USSR)	18.85
3 U. Schorn (FGR)	18.70

1974 WORLD CHAMPIONSHIPS
Men
Combined exercises

	Marks
1 S. Kasamatsu (Japan)	116.10
2 N. Andrianov (USSR)	114.95
3 E. Kenmotsu (Japan)	114.50

Floor

1 S. Kasamatsu (Japan)	19.375
2 H. Kajiyama (Japan)	19.325
3 A. Keranov (Bulg)	19.225

High bar	Marks
1 E. Gienger (FGR)	19.500
2 W. Thune (GDR)	19.450
3 {E. Kenmotsu (Japan) / A. Szajna (Poland)	19.275

Parallel bars

1 E. Kenmotsu (Japan)	19.375
2 N. Andrianov (USSR)	19.325
3 V. Marchenko (USSR)	18.850

Pommel horse

1 Z. Magyar (Hun)	19.575
2 N. Andrianov (USSR)	19.375
3 E. Kenmotsu (Japan)	19.225

Rings

1 {N. Andrianov (USSR) / D. Grecu (Romania)	19.525
3 A. Szajna (Poland)	19.225

Vault

1 S. Kasamatsu (Japan)	19.325
2 N. Andrianov (USSR)	19.250
3 H. Kajiyama (Japan)	19.225

Team

1 Japan	571.40
2 USSR	567.35
3 GDR	562.40

Women
Combined exercises

1 L. Tourischeva (USSR)	78.450
2 O. Korbut (USSR)	77.650
3 A. Hellmann (GDR)	76.875

Bars

1 A. Zinke (GDR)	19.650
2 O. Korbut (USSR)	19.575
3 L. Tourischeva (USSR)	19.500

Beam

1 L. Tourischeva (USSR)	19.725
2 O. Korbut (USSR)	19.525
3 N. Kim (USSR)	19.200

Floor

1 L. Tourischeva (USSR)	19.775
2 O. Korbut (USSR)	19.600
3 {E. Saadi (USSR) / R. Siharulidze (USSR)	19.550

Vault	Marks
1 O. Korbut (USSR)	19.450
2 L. Tourischeva (USSR)	19.200
3 B. Perdykulova (Czech)	19.075

Team	
1 USSR	384.15
2 GDR	376.55
3 Hungary	370.60

1975 EUROPEAN CHAMPIONSHIPS

Men

Combined exercises	Marks
1 N. Andrianov (USSR)	57.90
2 E. Gienger (FGR)	56.85
3 A. Detiatin (USSR)	56.70

Floor

1 { N. Andrianov (USSR) / A. Szajna (Poland) }	19.15
3 J. Tabak (Czech)	19.05

High bar

1 { N. Andrianov (USSR) / E. Gienger (FGR) }	19.50
3 A. Szajna (Poland)	19.10

Parallel bars

1 N. Andrianov (USSR)	19.40
2 A. Detiatin (USSR)	18.95
3 V. Klimenko (USSR)	18.75

Pommel horse

1 Z. Magyar (Hun)	19.50
2 A. Andrianov (USSR)	19.40
3 E. Gienger (FGR)	19.05

Rings

1 D. Grecu (Romania)	19.60
2 M. Bors (Romania)	19.30
3 A. Detiatin (USSR)	19.15

Vaults

1 N. Andrianov (USSR)	19.02
2 A. Detiatin (USSR)	18.95
3 J. Tabak (Czech)	18.77

Women

Combined exercises	
1 N. Comaneci (Romania)	38.85
2 N. Kim (USSR)	38.50
3 A. Zinke (GDR)	37.95

Bars	Marks
1 N. Comaneci (Romania)	19.65
2 A. Zinke (GDR)	19.55
3 N. Kim (USSR)	19.50

Beam

1 N. Comaneci (Romania)	19.50
2 N. Kim (USSR)	19.15
3 A. Goreac (Romania)	19.00

Floor

1 N. Kim (USSR)	19.55
2 N. Comaneci (Romania)	19.40
3 L. Tourischeva (USSR)	19.35

Vault

1 N. Comaneci (Romania)	19.50
2 R. Schmeisser (GDR)	19.10
3 { A. Goreac (Romania) / N. Kim (USSR) }	19.00

1975 WORLD CUP

Men

Combined exercises	Marks
1 N. Andrianov (USSR)	56.35
2 H. Kajiyama (Japan)	56.20
3 A. Detiatin (USSR)	55.90

Floor

1 H. Kajiyama (Japan)	18.90
2 N. Andrianov (USSR)	18.75
3 V. Safronov (USSR)	18.70

High bar

1 M. Tsukahara (Japan)	19.45
2 E. Gienger (FGR)	19.35
3 H. Kajiyama (Japan)	19.20

Parallel bars

1 N. Andrianov (USSR)	19.10
2 { H. Kajiyama (Japan) / M. Tsukahara (Japan) }	19.00

Pommel horse

1 Z. Magyar (Hun)	19.40
2 N. Andrianov (USSR)	19.00
3 H. Kajiyama (Japan)	18.85

Rings

1 M. Tsukahara (Japan)	19.05
2 F. Honma (Japan)	18.85
3 D. Grecu (Romania)	18.75

Vault

	Marks
1 P. Shamugia (USSR)	19.05
2 H. Kajiyama (Japan)	19.025
3 V. Safronov (USSR)	19.00

Women
Combined exercises

1 L. Tourischeva (USSR)	39.15
2 O. Korbut (USSR)	38.55
3 { M. Egervari (Hun) { E. Saadi (USSR)	38.30

Bars

1 L. Tourischeva (USSR)	19.50
2 L. Gorbik (USSR)	19.30
3 E. Saadi (USSR)	19.20

Beam

1 L. Tourischeva (USSR)	19.45
2 M. Egervari (Hun)	19.15
3 E. Saadi (USSR)	19.05

Floor

1 L. Tourischeva (USSR)	19.60
2 { E. Saadi (USSR) { T. Ungureanu (Romania)	19.40

Vault

1 L. Tourischeva (USSR)	19.35
2 { O. Koval (USSR) { E. Saadi (USSR)	19.15

1976 OLYMPIC GAMES
Men
Combined exercises

	Marks
1 N. Andrianov (USSR)	116.65
2 S. Kato (Japan)	115.65
3 M. Tsukahara (Japan)	115.575

Floor

1 N. Andrianov (USSR)	19.45
2 V. Marchenko (USSR)	19.425
3 P. Kormann (USA)	19.30

High bar

1 M. Tsukahara (Japan)	19.675
2 E. Kenmotsu (Japan)	19.50
3 E. Gienger (FGR)	19.475

Parallel bars

1 S. Kato (Japan)	19.675
2 N. Andrianov (USSR)	19.50
3 M. Tsukahara (Japan)	19.475

Pommel horse

1 Z. Magyar (Hun)	19.70
2 E. Kenmotsu (Japan)	19.575
3 N. Andrianov (USSR)	19.525

Rings

	Marks
1 N. Andrianov (USSR)	19.65
2 A. Ditiatin (USSR)	19.55
3 D. Grecu (Romania)	19.50

Vault

1 N. Andrianov (USSR)	19.45
2 M. Tsukahara (Japan)	19.375
3 H. Kajiyama (Japan)	19.275

Team

1 Japan	576.85
2 USSR	576.45
3 Germany	564.65

Women
Combined exercises

1 N. Comaneci (Romania)	79.275
2 N. Kim (USSR)	78.675
3 L. Tourischeva (USSR)	78.625

Bars

1 N. Comaneci (Romania)	20.00
2 T. Ungureanu (Romania)	19.80
3 M. Egervari (Hun)	19.775

Beam

1 N. Comaneci (Romania)	19.95
2 O. Korbut (USSR)	19.725
3 T. Ungureanu (Romania)	19.70

Floor

1 N. Kim (USSR)	19.85
2 L. Tourischeva (USSR)	19.825
3 N. Comaneci (Romania)	19.75

Vault

1 N. Kim (USSR)	19.80
2 L. Tourischeva (USSR)	19.65
3 C. Dombeck (GDR)	19.65

Team

1 USSR	390.35
2 Romania	387.15
3 GDR	385.10

1977 EUROPEAN CHAMPIONSHIPS
Men
Combined exercises

	Marks
1 V. Markelov (USSR)	57.80
2 A. Tkachev (USSR)	57.25
3 V. Tikhonov (USSR)	56.85

Floor

1 A. Tkachev (USSR)	19.30
2 V. Markelov (USSR)	19.15
3 V. Tikhonov (USSR)	19.10

High bar	Marks
1 S. Deltchev (Bulg)	19.35
2 {V. Markelov (USSR) / A. Tkachev (USSR)	19.25

Parallel bars	
1 V. Tikhonov (USSR)	19.10
2 {R. Barthel (GDR) / E. Gienger (FRG)	18.90

Pommel horse	
1 Z. Magyar (Hun)	19.80
2 M. Nikolai (GDR)	19.55
3 V. Markelov (USSR)	19.35

Rings	
1 V. Markelov (USSR)	19.60
2 A. Tkachev (USSR)	19.40
3 V. Tikhonov (USSR)	19.15

Vault	
1 {R. Barthel (GDR) / J. Tabak (Czech)	19.275
3 V. Markelov (USSR)	19.050

Women

Combined exercises	
1 N. Comaneci (Romania)	39.30
2 E. Moukhina (USSR)	38.95
3 N. Kim (USSR)	38.85

Bars	
1 {N. Comaneci (Romania) / E. Moukhina (USSR)	19.650
3 S. Kraker (GDR)	19.600

Beam	
1 E. Moukhina (USSR)	19.400
2 N. Kim (USSR)	19.350
3 M. Filatova (USSR)	19.250

Floor	
1 {M. Filatova (USSR) / E. Moukhina (USSR)	19.700
3 N. Kim (USSR)	19.550

Vault	
1 N. Kim (USSR)	19.525
2 N. Comaneci (Romania)	19.500
3 E. Moukhina (USSR)	19.450

1977 WORLD CUP
Men

Combined exercises	Marks
1 {N. Andrianov (USSR) / V. Markelov (USSR)	57.45
3 A. Tkachev (USSR)	57.35

Floor	Marks
1 N. Andrianov (USSR)	19.25
2 A. Tkachev (USSR)	19.00
3 V. Markelov (USSR)	18.95

High bar	
1 {E. Gienger (GDR) / V. Markelov (USSR) / A. Tkachev (USSR)	19.60

Parallel bars	
1 N. Andrianov (USSR)	19.20
2 A. Tkachev (USSR)	19.15
3 S. Kato (Japan)	19.10

Pommel horse	
1 {V. Markelov (USSR) / M. Nikolai (GDR)	19.50
3 A. Tkachev (USSR)	19.15

Rings	
1 N. Andrianov (USSR)	19.70
2 V. Markelov (USSR)	19.55
3 A. Tkachev (USSR)	19.45

Vault	
1 V. Markelov (USSR)	19.15
2 N. Andrianov (USSR)	19.05
3 R. Bruckner (GDR)	18.95

Women

Combined exercises	
1 M. Filatova (USSR)	38.95
2 S. Kraker (GDR)	38.45
3 N. Shaposhnikova (USSR)	38.20

Bars	
1 E. Moukhina (USSR)	19.60
2 M. Filatova (USSR)	19.45
3 S. Kraker (GDR)	19.40

Beam	
1 E. Moukhina (USSR)	19.30
2 S. Kraker (GDR)	19.00
3 A. Grigoras (Romania)	18.85

Floor	
1 M. Filatova (USSR)	19.70
2 {V. Cerna (Czech) / S. Kraker (GDR)	19.25

Vault	
1 N. Shaposhnikova (USSR)	19.425
2 M. Filatova (USSR)	19.35
3 M. Egervari (Hun)	19.05

1978 COMMONWEALTH GAMES

Men

Combined exercises	Marks
1 P. Delesalle (Canada)	56.40
2 L. Mylund (Australia)	54.95
3 J. Choquett (Canada)	54.25

Team

1 Canada	165.55
2 England	161.95
3 Australia	158.50

Women

Combined exercises	
1 E. Schlegel (Canada)	38.25
2 { S. Hawco (Canada) M. Goermann (Canada)	37.65

Team

1 Canada	113.25
2 England	107.40
3 New Zealand	106.35

Bibliography

Freestanding by G. C. Kunzle & B. W. Thomas (James Barrie, London; 1956)

Horizontal Bar by G. C. Kunzle (James Barrie, London; 1957)

Pommel Horse by G. C. Kunzle (Barrie & Rockliff, London; 1960)

Activities on P.E. Apparatus by J. Edmundson & J. Garstang (Oldbourne, London; 1962)

Competitive Gymnastics by Nik Stuart (Stanley Paul, London; 1964)

Parallel Bars by G. C. Kunzle (Barrie & Rockliff, London; 1964)

Trampolining by D. E. Horne (Faber & Faber, London; 1968)

Gymnastics for Girls and Women by E. R. Carter (Prentice-Hall, New Jersey; 1969)

Olympic Gymnastics for Men and Women by B. Taylor, B. Bajin & T. Zivic (Prentice Hall, New Jersey; 1972)

Rules of the Game ed. by The Diagram Group (Paddington Press, USA & UK; 1974)

Oxford Companion to Sports and Games ed. by John Arlott (Oxford University Press, London; 1975)

An Introduction to Modern Rhythmic Gymnastics by Jenny Bott (B.A.G.A.: 1976)

Enjoying Gymnastics ed. by The Diagram Group (Paddington Press, USA & UK; 1976)

Olympic Gymnastics by Akitomo Kaneko (Sterling Publishing Co., New York; 1976)

The Olympic Games ed. by John Rodda & Lord Killanin (Barrie & Jenkins, London; 1976)

Gymnastics for Girls by Frank Ryan (Viking Press, USA, 1976; Penguin Books, UK; 1977)

Better Gymnastics by Pauline Prestidge (Kaye & Ward, London; 1977)

Gymnastics Safety Manual ed. by E. Wettstone (Pennsylvania State University Press; 1977)

Nadia of Romania by Marion Connock (Duckworth, London; 1977)

Gymnastics for Girls by C. Temple & P. Tatlow (Pelham Books, London; 1977)

Gymnastics for Men by Nik Stuart (Stanley Paul, London; 1978)

Though by no means the only books written on the subject in recent years, these are among those I found most helpful.

D.H.

Glossary

Amplitude highly-desirable quality indicating that movements are fully and freely expressed.

Bridge backward arch of the body achieved by letting the feet fall from a handstand.

Cross static demonstration of strength on the rings, in which the arms are extended horizontally and the body remains vertical.

Croup part of the long vaulting horse nearest to the performer; part of the pommel horse on his right.

Diomidov advanced stunt on parallel bars in which the performer turns 360 degrees into a handstand from a forward swing.

Dislocation grip in which the body hangs, from bar or rings, with the arms behind the back.

Drop the return of the body to a trampoline bed.

Flic-flac a back handspring, or back flip; seen on floor or beam.

Hang when the body is entirely below bars or rings (the opposite to 'support').

Hecht 'swallow dive' attitude seen in vault of that name, and in similar dismount from asymmetric bars.

Hip circle revolution around a bar in which the body is kept close to it, at hip level.

Kip common means of raising the body from any kind of hang position directly to any kind of support position.

Layout full extension of the body, seen in swings and somersaults.

Mill circle revolution of a high or asymmetric bar in which the legs are astride and the bar between them.

Neck part of the long vaulting horse furthest from the performer; part of the pommel horse on his left.

Pike produced by raising the extended legs towards the trunk, often to a very acute angle.

Planche advanced demonstration of strength plus balance in which the body is supported horizontally entirely on the hands.

Pyramid human tower built during group exercises in sports acrobatics.

Radochla somersault between the asymmetric bars, developed by East German gymnast.

Reuther board most common type of springboard, used in vaulting etc.

Roundoff Popular tumbling move in which the body twists 180 degrees as it rotates forward 360 degrees.

Saddle centre section of the pommel horse.

Safety belt means of controlling and protecting the gymnast during practice.

Scale one-legged balancing pose.

Ski run sprung platform for the perfomance of solo tumbling exercises.

Sole circle revolution on high or asymmetric bars in which the feet, as well as the hands, remain on the bar.

Spotter essential attendant at all apparatus practice, for safety and for coaching. At least two needed at a trampoline.

Stalder difficult trick named after Swiss high bar expert.

Stoop vault in which the performer's body is bent forward as his feet pass over the horse.

Straddle the spreading wide of the legs, during vaulting etc.

Strelli a handstand on the parallel bars reached through a backward roll.

Stutze parallel bars stunt in which the gymnast turns 180 degrees during a forward support swing.

Support basic position used on much apparatus, in which the shoulders are above the hands and the arms straight, taking the whole weight of the body.

Tinsica move similar to a forward walk-over, in which the hands (and feet) reach the ground, or the beam, one at a time.

Travel movement of the gymnast from the saddle of the pommel horse to either end, or vice versa.

Tuck position commonly seen in somersaults, in which the knees are brought as close as possible to the chest.

Tsukahara vault incorporating 180-degree preflight turn and 540-degree postflight somersault (Japanese gymnast).

Uprise method of raising the body from hang to support by means of swing.

Walkover on the floor or beam, a move in which the body passes through a handstand to a 360-degree rotation (forward or backward); free (or aerial) walkover, one without using the hands.

Wheel (or giant circle, or giant swing) circle of high bar with arms and body fully extended.

Wrap move on asymmetric bars in which the gymnast, swinging from the high bar, meets the low one at hip level.

Yamashita handspring vault with pike, named after Japanese gymnast who created it.

Index